HD
69
N4
P32

Park, William R.

Strategic analysis
for venture
evaluations

DATE			

Strategic Analysis For Venture Evaluation:

The SAVE Approach to Business Decisions

Strategic Analysis For Venture Evaluation:

The SAVE Approach
to Business Decisions

W. R. Park and J. B. Maillie

VNR VAN NOSTRAND REINHOLD COMPANY
NEW YORK CINCINNATI TORONTO LONDON MELBOURNE

Van Nostrand Reinhold Company Regional Offices:
New York   Cincinnati

Van Nostrand Reinhold Company International Offices:
London   Toronto   Melbourne

Library of Congress Catalog Card Number: 81-1205
ISBN: 0-442-24507-6

Manufactured in the United States of America

Published by Van Nostrand Reinhold Company
135 West 50th Street, New York, N.Y. 10020

Published simultaneously in Canada by Van Nostrand Reinhold Ltd.

15   14   13   12   11   10   9   8   7   6   5   4   3   2   1

Library of Congress Cataloging in Publication Data

Park, William R.
    Strategic analysis for venture evaluation.

    Includes index.
    1. New products—Evaluation. 2. New business
enterprises—Evaluation. I. Maillie, J. B.
II. Title. III. Title: Venture evaluation.
HD69.N4P32   658.4'06   81-1205
ISBN 0-442-24507-6   AACR2

The Planning Options

I have three options, three options have I—
Improve, expand and diversify.
There aren't any others (except one, you know—
The deadly acceptance of status quo).

J. B. Maillie
1972

A Graveyard of Overriding Considerations

Here lies a venture that was doomed to fail
　From the moment its sponsors decided to sail
Without a good look at all factors involved.
　They simply pressed forward, firmly resolved.

"Very timely," said one. Another said, "Clever."
　"Could it miss?" someone asked. The chorus roared, "Never!"
One aspect alone caused them all to adore it:
　And this was the fact that the Old Man was for it.

And there is the grave of another sure bet—
　Had a twenty-claim patent, the best written yet.
They tooled up and turned out a million to try it—
　Before users convinced them they just wouldn't buy it.

Over here lies a merger they said would provide
　Tax loss protection for profits inside.
But all the king's horses and all the king's men
　Couldn't stop it from losing again and again.

The ghosts of these ventures cry out in the night,
　"We're all here because of some clear oversight.
Way back at the start, the causes of trouble
　Were as easy to see as the sun through a bubble.

"In most of the cases, the firms were aware
　Of the negative factors that lurked everywhere.
They could have avoided the failure and mayhem—
　They *knew* all the factors, but they just didn't weigh 'em."

J. B. Maillie
1970

Foreword

I was pleased to be asked to write a Foreword to *Strategic Analysis* by Bill Park and Jeff Maillie on their analytical process for venture evaluations. These two men, without question, stand in the forefront of innovative and imaginative researchers in this country. Their individual and joint efforts over the years clearly demonstrated that scientific analysis and the scientific process could be applied to the art of business management. The scientific analytical processes familiar to all of us, if leavened with a strong touch of pragmatism and practical business psychology, do have a role in modern venture decision making—in areas far beyond their accepted use in conventional financial evaluations. The many successful projects managed by Bill Park and Jeff Maillie, where such analyses were a critical factor in the program, provide highly visible examples of such an application.

Jeff Maillie, the co-author of this book, passed away a short time ago. Jeff was a brilliant, practical researcher. His contributions to the Midwest Research Institute, and to the field of management research were enormous. He died before realizing his own full potential—but only because his potential was so great. The mark he left on the people who knew him is indelible. Equally important, the techniques and systems he developed for his research are as valid and useful today as they were when he created and refined them.

Bill Park is another truly remarkable individual. An author, a businessman, a researcher, a scholar, an engineer—Bill is all of these, and more. He was a colleague of Jeff Maillie, and the two of them developed the material that has led to the SAVE approach to business decision making.

The SAVE process is not a theoretical concept, or part of an academic exercise. It is a practical, realistic approach to venture analysis. It is a thoroughly tested, working methodology—having been applied successfully in both large and small businesses, and in a variety of other organizations.

I strongly urge any manager facing a venture-oriented decision to review carefully the material in this book, and consider the application of the SAVE approach to his own evaluation analysis. The manager who does so—and his company or organization—is certain to benefit.

John C. McKelvey
President, Midwest Research Institute
Kansas City, Missouri

Preface

Most venturers, whether individual entrepreneurs or large corporations, have poor results when it comes to choosing potential successes from the venture opportunities which are open to them. On the average, their choices are failures four out of five times.

Nevertheless, venture success or failure is highly predictable at a very early stage of evaluation, even before there need be any substantial capital commitment. The astonishing thing, though, is that present knowledge is usually adequate to predict venture outcome with remarkable accuracy. The biggest problem is the failure to make full use of the existing knowledge about a proposed venture or project, simply because the available facts and factors have not been collected, organized, and applied to the problem at hand.

Instead, proposals tend to be weighed in terms of a few major considerations—a timely tax shelter, an attractive patent, a promising payout calculation, a persuasive proponent, or enthusiastic sponsorship by the chief executive—exciting expectations which make balanced judgment nearly impossible. Much of what is known is ignored. Thousands of ventures fail each year for reasons which could have been recognized from their very beginnings.

Consequently, the SAVE technique—Strategic Analysis for Venture Evaluation—was developed. SAVE provides a highly effective means of gauging potential venture success in advance, by incorporating a number of "bite-sized" judgments about the factors that ultimately determine the venture's success or failure.

Every proposed venture, regardless of the type, has four broad facets that require exploration and evaluation: the *Item* (product, service, or action) which is involved, the *Company* (or in some cases, the individual entrepreneur), the *Environment,* and certain overall aspects of the *Venture* itself.

The SAVE model breaks down these four facets into 13 *General Aspects,* which in turn are divided into 69 *Individual Factors* that influence venture results. In preliminary screening evaluations, where many proposals or ideas are being rough-processed at one time, each proposal is rated numerically on a scale of 1 to 10 with respect to each of the 13 general aspects. During a full evaluation—such as that required for the final selection of the best proposal from among several screened candidates—each proposal is rated from 1 to 10 on each of the 69 individual factors. The model can be easily adapted to virtually any situation, recognizing the uniqueness of every company, every environment, and every venture.

SAVE provides a clearly stated frame of reference for each judgment it requires. In the ratings, *one* is always the worst, the most unfavorable with reference to a stated norm such as average competition, represented by a rating of *five*. A *ten* is always the best or most desirable. The evaluator chooses any rating from one to ten which best measures his judgment according to the particular scale which is described for each individual factor. The resulting ratings enable management to judge the merits of all proposals more accurately and meaningfully, showing how good or how bad a proposal is, compared with familiar standards.

Thus, SAVE enables a company to make maximum use of one of its most valuable assets—its present knowledge—and apply it effectively to one of the toughest problems encountered anywhere in business: the evaluation of proposed new ventures.

SAVE compels thoughtful attention to *all* factors involved in a venture, thereby eliminating dangerous blind spots. Along with this, it prevents overvaluing a few dominant considerations that tend to distort decision judgment.

At the same time, SAVE significantly reduces the chances of venture failure by pinpointing potential future dangers in the very beginning. It also identifies and quantifies strengths and weaknesses in present operations, thus offering the opportunity to tailor venture selections for specific strategic purposes. And it shows exactly where the available information is too weak for reliable evaluations, enabling further efforts to be directed toward specific needs.

Altogether, the SAVE approach, through its accurate, practical, and structured evaluation capability, provides a sound and consistent basis for comparing the merits of various proposals with each other, for relating a proposed venture to the known results of a firm's present activities, and for predicting the chances of success for an entirely new enterprise.

W. R. Park
J. B. Maillie

Contents

ILLUSTRATIONS

TABLES

Strategic Analysis For Venture Evaluation:

The SAVE Approach
to Business Decisions

1
An Introduction to Strategic Analysis

Looking back over the years at many cases of business venture failure, one striking observation can be made: in the overwhelming majority of cases, failures can be predicted in advance. In fact, more than 90 percent of all business failures can be traced and attributed directly to causes known in advance. Known, but ignored.

Even the 12,000 to 15,000 bankruptcies reported each year probably represent only a small corner in the huge graveyard of total venture failures. Most failing ventures are never reported as such, but are instead simply loss entries on otherwise healthy income statements, projects abandoned quietly after substantial investments. Many other projects "succeed" only by the grace of indulgent accounting practices, or else as 10-, 12-, or 15-year payouts.

While nine out of ten business venture failures can, by virtue of hindsight, be attributed to previously known causes, it seems safe to assume that at least one-half, and possibly three-fourths, of all venture failures can be responsibly predicted in advance. Also, a large portion of them might not be undertaken at all if the odds against their success can be accurately established before any large sums of money are committed.

The reasons for failure are almost never subtle, and they seldom represent any actual *mis*judgments. The reasons are generally well-known, but they usually go unjudged in any really objective or analytical sense. They are simply ignored in favor of certain overriding considerations. The proposed item is believed to have a great patent, a good captive sales volume, an attractive tax situation, an apparently terrific payout, or some other exciting aspects which make a balanced judgment impossible.

Such "inclined judgments" receive little help at most banks if the venture involves a commercial loan. Loan officers are among the most venture-exposed persons to be found anywhere in business, but the value of their broad experience is generally confined strictly to the financial aspects of a new venture. This unfortunate constraint deprives many firms of one of their best potential sources of objectivity in venture evaluation.

Convincing evidence can be compiled to show that most companies already have sufficient latent knowledge to be able to prejudge the relative success of most new ventures with remarkable accuracy. It is largely a matter of collecting, organizing, and properly utilizing the organization's best information, experience, and judgment, and confirming with research only when necessary.

Simple, yet unique, methods have been developed for putting the already-available information together into a manageable form, so that management judgments can be applied in an orderly and objective fashion. The SAVE approach—Strategic Analysis for Venture Evaluation—is an evolution or refinement of two earlier approaches: (1) VERS, the Venture Evaluation Rating System and (2) SCET, a Scaled Comparison Evaluation Technique.

VERS: VENTURE EVALUATION RATING SYSTEM

VERS is an extremely simple concept, yet it is flexible enough to be applied to virtually any type of new business venture. It employs the concept of a three-legged stool, with the seat representing the new product or new business profits. The three legs then represent the major factors required to support these profits. Figure 1-1 illustrates the basic idea behind the VERS approach.

In Fig. 1-1, the three supporting legs depict the product, the company, and the market. The only assurance of success for a new venture is strength and balance in all three legs. A strong company cannot expect to succeed with an inferior product, or even with a good product for which there is no market. Similarly, a superior product having a strong market potential cannot succeed if the company lacks the marketing, technical, or production know-how that can get the product on the market and to its market.

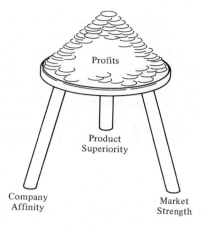

Fig. 1-1. The VERS concept.

Just recognizing these three factors before getting into a new business venture, and objectively evaluating them before making any major financial commitments, can be the most important decision made in avoiding a major financial disaster. The procedure is so simple and quick that there is absolutely no excuse for not following through with it. Even so, thousands of ventures are entered into supported only by the emotional enthusiasm of those individuals most interested in them. These individuals fail to realize that others—their market—do not share the same enthusiasm, or that the world will not beat a path to their door (or even cross the street in heavy traffic) to buy their product unless it possesses overwhelming superiority over all competitive products in terms of performance or salability.

The chances of success for a new product or a new business venture can be predicted with a fair degree of accuracy, simply by looking at each of the three major factors: the product (or merchandise or service) to be sold, the market to which it is to be sold, and the ability of the company to match the product to the market. By rating each factor relative to competitive businesses, products, and markets, some of the emotional involvement can be eliminated or at least minimized. Each factor should be rated as being either superior to, equal to, or not as good as the competition.

Obviously, the best chance of success goes to the new venture involving a superior product, offered by a strong company in a market having good volume, growth, stability, and competitive characteristics. Conversely, an untested product offered by a new company in an unknown market has very little chance of success. Table 1-1 shows how the chances of success for a new business venture—whether manufacturing, retail or service—might vary, depending on how the three key factors are rated, relative to competition.

Effective as it may be, this approach is obviously open to considerable refinement. The next step incorporates more factors, and assigns different weights to the factors. This becomes the SCET approach.

Table 1-1. Chances of success for new business venture.

| | Factor Being Rated | | |
Product Superiority	Company Affinity	Market Strength	Relative Chance of Success
+	+	+	100
+	+	=	63
+	+	−	25
+	=	+	63
+	=	=	39
+	=	−	16
+	−	+	25
+	−	=	16
+	−	−	6
=	+	+	63
=	+	=	39
=	+	−	16
=	=	+	39
=	=	=	24
=	=	−	10
=	−	+	16
=	−	=	10
=	−	−	4
−	+	+	25
−	+	=	16
−	+	−	6
−	=	+	16
−	=	=	10
−	=	−	4
−	−	+	6
−	−	=	4
−	−	−	1

Rating Scale: + represents good or better than average competition; = represents average, or equal to competition; − designates poor, or worse than competition.

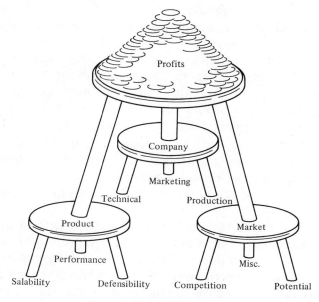

Fig. 1-2. The SCET concept.

SCET: SCALED COMPARISON EVALUATION TECHNIQUE

The SCET approach recognizes the presence of a number of factors affecting the three major elements of new business venture success: (1) the product, (2) the company, and (3) the market. Instead of a single three-legged stool, each leg of the original stool is resting on another three-legged stool, each of whose legs are again supported by three additional factors. Thus, the SCET approach employs a total of 27 specific factors that determine the success or failure of the new business venture. Figure 1-2 illustrates the next level of support.

Here, the *product* factors are divided into three broad categories: (1) *performance*, measured in terms of product efficiency, reliability, and convenience, (2) *salability*, determined by the product's uniqueness, attractiveness, and economy, and (3) *defensibility*, where the product is protected by patents, other proprietary considerations, or newness.

Next, the *company* factors are divided into three categories, each of which is defined by three subcategories: (1) *marketing*, a measure of the company's sales, distribution, and service capabilities, (2) *technology*, the firm's abilities to work with the necessary materials, techniques, and designs, and (3) *production*, the firm's labor, facilities, and strategic resources.

Finally, the *market* factors must be assessed, again by breaking them down into three categories each containing three factors: (1) market *potential*, based on the market volume, growth, and stability, (2) the *competition*, how well it is entrenched, the capital structure of the industry, and overall price levels established for competitive products, and (3) a *miscellaneous* category, covering such items as the group position, special threats, and intuitive feelings regarding the new product or venture.

A typical work sheet used in the SCET analysis is shown in Fig. 1-3.

The 27-factor SCET model offers an orderly method of appraising the relative merits of a proposed new venture and judging its prospects of successful pursuit by a given company under the existing economic and competitive conditions. While the SCET approach was originally developed for use in the metal fabricating industries, when appropriately interpreted it also has virtually unlimited application in other kinds of industries. Its great versatility permits tailoring evaluations to fit any size and type of venture proposal with appropriate depth and effort—ranging from 20-minute "eye-ball" appraisals to formal and sophisticated programs to provide evaluation services for large companies on a continuing basis.

In the SCET evaluation, each of the 27 factors is rated independently, preferably by several knowledgeable individuals involved or to be involved in the proposed venture should it prove worth pursuing. For example, in a large corporation, the evaluation group might include representatives of the firm's research, production, financial, marketing, and other appropriately involved management functions. In a small company, the evaluation might be conducted informally by only a few individuals. It is important, though, to have at least two separate opinions in the SCET analysis, even if they involve only a husband and wife team or two partners.

In conducting the evaluation, each of the 27 factors will be assigned a point score ranging between 0 and 10. A score of 10 points for a factor indicates an unquestionable level of perfection or superiority, resulting in a tremendous competitive advantage in that area,

Item _____

Date _____

Evaluated By _____

Rate From 0 To 10:

Efficiency   *_____ ⎫
Reliability   *_____ ⎬ Performance _____ ⎫
Convenience   _____ ⎭   ⎪
                                                ⎬
Uniqueness   _____ ⎫   ⎪
Attractiveness   *_____ ⎬ Salability _____ ⎬ Product _____ ⎫
Economy   _____ ⎭   ⎪   ⎪
                                                ⎪   ⎪
Patent   _____ ⎫   ⎪   ⎪
Proprietary   _____ ⎬ Defensibility _____ ⎭   ⎪
Newness   _____ ⎭   ⎪
                                                                ⎪
Sales   _____ ⎫   ⎪
Distribution   _____ ⎬ Marketing   _____ ⎫   ⎪
Service   _____ ⎭   ⎪   ⎪
                                                ⎪   ⎪
Materials   _____ ⎫   ⎪   ⎬ Total
Techniques   _____ ⎬ Technical   _____ ⎬ Company _____ ⎬ Rating
Design   _____ ⎭   ⎪   ⎪   ◯
                                                ⎪   ⎪
Labor   _____ ⎫   ⎪   ⎪
Facilities   _____ ⎬ Production _____ ⎭   ⎪
Strategy   _____ ⎭   ⎪
                                                                ⎪
Volume   _____ ⎫   ⎪
Growth   _____ ⎬ Potential   _____ ⎫   ⎪
Stability   _____ ⎭   ⎪   ⎪
                                                ⎪   ⎪
Capital   *_____ ⎫   ⎪   ⎪
Prices   *_____ ⎬ Competition _____ ⎬ Market _____ ⎭
Entrenchment   _____ ⎭   ⎪
                                                ⎪
Group Position   _____ ⎫   ⎪
Special Threats   _____ ⎬ Miscellaneous _____ ⎭
Intuition   _____ ⎭

*Zero rating eliminates item from further consideration.

General Comment _____
_____
_____
_____

Fig. 1-3. SCET work sheet.

clearly ahead of and easily maintained over all others in the field. A score of 0, on the other hand, describes an obvious, serious, and perhaps overwhelming competitive disadvantage. A score of 5 reflects a position generally equal to competition, without any discernable advantages or disadvantages.

Should the proposed new venture receive a total score of 270—the maximum possible—from all those evaluating it, the project is an obvious, unqualified winner. This would be comparable to playing 18 holes of golf in 18 strokes, and would be about equally probable. At the other extreme, a score of 0 in the SCET analysis would be an equally obvious disaster; anything this bad would be unlikely to have even reached the evaluation stage.

As with most important business decisions, many proposals will fall in a category that looks almost too good to pass up, but not quite good enough to pursue. Mediocrity is always difficult to evaluate.

While it is possible to formulate a policy that says, for example, to pursue projects that score 80 percent or more and to abandon those that score less, the primary value of the SCET method is rarely to provide an immediate "go—no go" decision. Instead, it serves better in selecting the most promising of several available opportunities, or in identifying the potential strengths and weaknesses of a new project before committing any more money to it. In many cases, a weak project can be strengthened with relative ease, providing its specific weaknesses can be identified in advance. SCET makes the identification easy, or at least possible.

Should any of the 27 SCET factors be considered entirely inappropriate for or irrelevant to the proposal being evaluated, these factors can be disregarded and excluded from the analysis. A percentage score can be obtained by dividing the total SCET score—or the average of the several scores given by those performing the analysis—by the maximum score possible (270 or less, depending on whether certain factors are excluded). The resulting percentage can be interpreted as an indication of the project's chances for success.

This 27-factor approach has worked well for many types of projects in a wide variety of industries. The next refinement to the SCET approach involves the addition of new factors and the introduction of a number of specific adjustments. This "third-generation" evaluation procedure is SAVE.

THE SAVE APPROACH—STRATEGIC ANALYSIS FOR VENTURE EVALUATION

The general approach to the SAVE technique is essentially similar to the SCET technique described in the preceding section. SAVE, however, incorporates 69 factors (compared to SCET's 27 factors), broken down into 4 major aspects (instead of 3), with 13 major factor groups (instead of nine). Also, provision is made in SAVE for 7 specific types of adjustments.

With the addition of the fourth major aspect, the three-legged stool was forced into retirement. However, the concept remains the same, with any new venture requiring both strength and balance in its four major aspects, as well as in the factors supporting these major aspects, in order to become successful.

SAVE can be viewed as a kind of businessman's pari-mutuel device: it will not tell the winner, or even how to bet, but it does tell a good deal about the odds. And, like a pari-mutuel, SAVE recognizes that increasing the investment in certain areas can help to improve the odds of success.

The feature that distinguishes SAVE from conventional evaluation systems is that it compels a multiplicity of individual judgment inputs, each with a known and clearly stated reference frame of its own. In effect, it constructs a mosaic pattern of bite-sized judgments and incorporates them into a comprehensive rating directly comparable with the ratings of other proposed ventures and with the company's present outputs. A rating for a given diversification proposal in February, for example, is directly comparable with a completely unrelated proposal in September; a proposed new product rating is directly comparable to those ratings, and also to the ratings of present products or past ventures, either successful or unsuccessful.

This intercomparability of ratings eliminates floating vacuum references like the one where a fellow asks, "How's your wife?" and is answered, "Compared to what?"

The SAVE model provides an excellent discipline for subjective evaluation by limiting exuberance and misgivings over certain factors to scales befitting their true importance, thereby making self-delusions quite obvious. Nevertheless, its greatest value may lie in the facility it provides for the gathering of a company's best elementary judgments for assimilation and orderly processing, either manually or by computer. In other words, SAVE transfers the company's aggregate experience and observation (in terms of subjective judgments) to a processor that interrelates this information in a completely objective manner while incorporating the various weighting and adjustment computations.

The basic SAVE model comprises four sections called *major aspects*. These include:

1. The particular *item* being proposed, the object of the venture in question,
2. The *company* itself,
3. The *environment*, and
4. The *venture* undertaking as a whole.

Each of these four major aspects is, in turn, subdivided into several *Factor Groups* (13 in all); and each factor group contains from three to nine *Factors*. There are 69 factors altogether, and they are placed in the model in patterns designed to provide proper weights for the various factor groups and major aspects. Figure 1-4 illustrates the overall structure of the SAVE model.

All of these factors are rated from 1 to 10 by each participating member of the company's management group, on each venture being proposed, and also on a selection of the company's present products or business activities. As many as seven different adjustments can be introduced for each rating. Considering that five persons might rate a half-dozen ventures or products on 69 factors having up to seven adjustments each—involving over 14,000 inputs—it is easy to understand why the job of processing the ratings may evolve into a computer problem.

Experience indicates that the SAVE approach is probably superior to any venture evaluation method presently in use in American business; this superiority comes mostly from the technique of using clearly stated frames of reference for the individual ratings (where a rating of one is worst, five is equal to competition, and ten denotes clear industry leadership) and for the composite ratings (compared with the known earning powers or other results of present products or ventures).

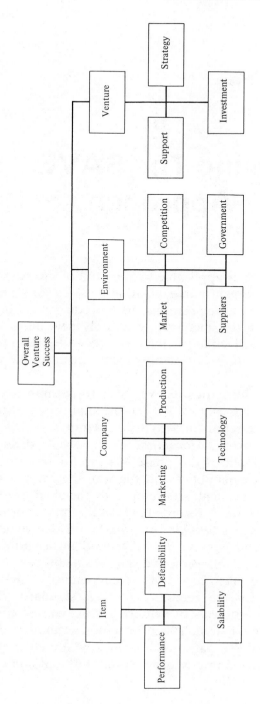

Fig. 1-4. The SAVE model.

2
Using The SAVE Approach

The SAVE approach is applicable to any kind of business and may be used to assist companies in evaluating a variety of types of ventures—diversifications, acquisitions, new products, major product changes, joint ventures, mergers, or entirely new businesses. The general approach will be much the same regardless of the type of venture involved, with specific adjustments ensuring the necessary realism.

A SAVE-based diversification venture, for example, might involve five distinct phases of effort: (1) formulation, (2) exploration, (3) evaluation, (4) selection, and (5) action planning.

The beginning involves *formulation* of a basic diversification strategy. The key input of this phase is a careful assessment of the company's present capabilities and the way they relate to the environment. This assessment is developed by the chief executive and operating managers and is recorded in SAVE terms according to the model's rating guide. A *company profile* should also be obtained at this time and should consist of background information such as earnings data, sales, employees, and special capabilities. This initial assessment enables construction of a comprehensive data base and reference models for the company—a basic standard framework against which the prospects of venture success can be consistently and meaningfully compared. The information accumulated here can be used to identify key patterns of company strengths and weaknesses to be considered in the formulation of an optimum diversification strategy. This strategy will guide the emphasis of subsequent research.

Should the formulated strategy call for a market-oriented diversification (a program aimed at exploiting a market need), the *exploration* phase will necessarily emphasize research to identify exploitable market needs. If the strategy calls for a capability-oriented diversification, the research emphasis aims at utilizing some form of unused capacity. A combination of the two is ideal, of course, because it assures a marketable operation with minimal investment. Another type of combination emphasis is one which both exploits a strength and reinforces a weakness. Occasionally, a firm is merely seeking a good (but perhaps unrelated) investment opportunity. Whatever the strategy might be, the objective of the exploration phase is to examine both markets and technology in sufficient depth to identify the most promising and appropriate diversification opportunities.

The number of prospective diversification ventures emerging from the exploration phase may be large or small, depending upon the type and size of the project. Various possibilities must be progressively screened to establish their eligibility for more and more detailed consideration.

The best of these possibilities, perhaps five or six items in number, are then *evaluated* in full 69-factor detail, using the best information, experience, and judgment available from within the company and from whatever additional sources are desired. The final candidates are then rated for careful comparison with each other and for analysis in terms of the company's present operations model. They will then be ranked in order according to: (1) their strategic merit, (2) security of investment, (3) profitability, or (4) other criteria as may be specified in the formulation phase of the project.

Selection is an obvious management responsibility. In cases where the company has good versatility or where an item fits present operations extremely well, the final choice may well have a higher score than most of the company's present outputs. Companies which are very narrowly specialized have less "venturability," and their proposals generally score lower than present outputs in every case.

Whatever the final selection, the company management will know exactly why it was chosen—how much better or how much worse than other proposals it was—in objective and rational terms. And they know a good deal more than that, because they have a complete picture of how it fits, where it is weak or strong, and by how much compared with competition. The system also pinpoints where additional information might be needed, so that any further research effort can be confined to highly specific items.

By the time a final selection is made, the project team has gained an excellent and well-organized understanding of the company, its operations and objectives, and considerable knowledge about the final choice itself. With only nominal supplemental research, the SAVE information can be used in *action planning* regarding organization for pursuit, point of entry, marketing strategy, and general program implementation.

Other·types of ventures are evaluated in exactly the same way. Prospective products are measured in terms facilitating direct comparison with each other and with present products. New product scores, incidentally, are usually accurate measures of relative profitability expectations. The reason, of course, is that profitability is determined by the same multiplicity of factors which structure the SAVE method. This thesis can be easily tested for validity in any individual company by simply rating the present products and comparing the results with actual profit records.

SAVE ADJUSTMENTS

In unadjusted form, SAVE may be thought of as a sort of fiscal profile. There are various adjustments, however, that make it possible to express the whole picture more meaningfully, in much the same way that a colored three-dimensional photograph tells a great deal more than a silhouette.

There are seven different types of adjustments involved in a full-depth SAVE project:

1. Standard industry division adjustments,
2. Venture displacement adjustments,
3. Certainty range specifications,
4. Judgment qualifications,
5. Judgment preference specifications,
6. Inclination adjustments, and
7. Special adjustments.

Proper use of some of these adjustments requires considerable professional knowledge and experience to avoid distortions and mis-interpretations. If the company lacks the necessary competence in this respect, then some of the adjustments should not be attempted. Obviously, an accurate and consistent silhouette is more reliable than a distorted and somewhat erratic photograph.

Standard Industry Division Adjustments. These adjustments are determined by the Standard Industrial Classification (SIC) Division code of the item's industry, as defined by the U.S. Department of Commerce. In the SAVE approach, the manufacturing industry evaluation model was designed to have a basic structural weight of one for each of the 69 factors rated. Major aspects and factor groups have various weights depending upon the number of factors they include. Factor weights in nonmanufacturing industries range from zero to three, depending upon their relative importance in the most typical cases, and their major aspect weights vary accordingly. Tables 2-1 through 2-4 show the factor weights for each of the 69 factors in each of nine industry groups.

If a manufacturer were evaluating a present or proposed manufactured item, he would use the indicated factor weights for the manufacturing industry for both the present and proposed items. If, however, he were evaluating a proposed venture into the transportation field, he would use the factor weights shown for the transportation industry in appraising the new venture; the resulting score could be compared to existing manufactured items, scored according to the factor weights listed for the manufacturing industry. The factors used in evaluating any specific venture, then, are weighted according to the industry in which that venture fits, and not according to the company's present industry.

Venture Displacement Adjustments. The relative importance of various factors is significantly affected by two things: (1) the general venture capability of the company (some organizations are simply more "venturable" than others) and (2) the magnitude of the basic differences between the present and proposed operations. The venture displacement adjustments take the form of factor weights to be applied to the specific factors affected, the weights ranging from one to five according to the venture displacement classification shown in Table 2-5.

Table 2-1. Item factor weights by industry.

	Industry Classification		
Factor	Agriculture	Mining	Contract Construction
Item			
Performance			
Effectiveness	2	1	1
Reliability	1	3	2
Simplicity	1	1	1
Convenience	1	1	1
Salability			
Appearance	1	1	1
Uniqueness	1	1	1
Economy	2	1	1
Timeliness	3	1	2
Understandability	1	1	1
Tradability	2	1	2
Buyability	1	1	1
Defensibility			
Legality	1	3	1
Newness	1	2	1
Proprietary	2	2	1

Factor	Manufacturing	Transportation	Wholesale and Retail Trade
Item			
Performance			
Effectiveness	1	1	1
Reliability	1	2	2
Simplicity	1	1	1
Convenience	1	2	3
Salability			
Appearance	1	2	1
Uniqueness	1	2	1
Economy	1	2	1
Timeliness	1	2	1
Understandability	1	2	2
Tradability	1	1	3
Buyability	1	1	2
Defensibility			
Legality	1	3	2
Newness	1	2	1
Proprietary	1	1	2

Table 2.1. Item factor weights by industry. (cont.)

	Industry Classification		
Factor	Finance, Insurance, Real Estate	Services	Government
Item			
Performance			
Effectiveness	1	1	1
Reliability	2	2	2
Simplicity	1	1	1
Convenience	2	2	1
Salability			
Appearance	1	1	2
Uniqueness	1	1	1
Economy	1	1	1
Timeliness	1	2	2
Understandability	1	2	1
Tradability	1	2	2
Buyability	2	2	1
Defensibility			
Legality	1	1	2
Newness	1	1	1
Proprietary	2	2	1

Table 2-2. Company factor weights by industry.

	Industry Classification		
Factor	Agriculture	Mining	Contract Construction
Company			
Marketing			
Experience	1	1	1
Support Services	1	1	1
Technical Service	1	1	1
Market Coverage	1	1	1
Entrenchment	1	1	3
Dependency	1	1	1
Volume	1	1	1
Penetration	1	1	1
Management	1	1	1
Technology			
Design	1	1	1
Engineering	1	2	1
Materials	2	3	1
Techniques	3	3	3
Production			
Labor	1	1	1
Facilities	1	2	1

Table 2-2. Company factor weights by industry. (cont.)

	Industry Classification		
Factor	Agriculture	Mining	Contract Construction
Purchasing	2	2	1
Dependency	1	1	1
Capacity	1	1	1
Location	2	2	1
Management	1	1	2

Factor	Manufacturing	Transportation	Wholesale and Retail Trade
Company			
Marketing			
Experience	1	1	2
Support Services	1	1	1
Technical Service	1	1	1
Market Coverage	1	1	1
Entrenchment	1	2	2
Dependency	1	1	1
Volume	1	1	1
Penetration	1	1	1
Management	1	1	1
Technology			
Design	1	1	1
Engineering	1	1	1
Materials	1	1	1
Techniques	1	2	1
Production			
Labor	1	1	1
Facilities	1	1	1
Purchasing	1	1	2
Dependency	1	1	1
Capacity	1	1	1
Location	1	2	2
Management	1	1	2

Factor	Finance, Insurance, Real Estate	Services	Government
Company			
Marketing			
Experience	1	2	2
Support Services	1	1	1
Technical Service	1	1	1
Market Coverage	1	1	1
Entrenchment	2	3	3
Dependency	1	1	1
Volume	1	1	1
Penetration	1	1	2
Management	2	2	1

Table 2-2. Company factor weights by industry. (cont.)

Industry Classification

Factor	Finance, Insurance, Real Estate	Services	Government
Technology			
Design	1	1	1
Engineering	1	1	1
Materials	1	1	1
Techniques	1	2	2
Production			
Labor	1	2	1
Facilities	1	1	1
Purchasing	1	1	1
Dependency	1	1	1
Capacity	1	1	1
Location	1	2	2
Management	1	1	1

Table 2-3. Environment factor weights by industry.

Industry Classification

Factor	Agriculture	Mining	Contract Construction
Environment			
Market			
Potential Volume	1	1	1
Proportion	1	1	1
Fertility	1	1	1
Growth	1	1	1
Stability	2	2	1
Outlook	1	1	1
Competition			
Size	2	3	2
Specialization	1	1	1
Entrenchment	1	1	1
Pricing	1	1	2
Entry Reaction	1	1	1
Suppliers			
Materials	2	1	2
Equipment	2	1	2
Services	2	2	2
Dependency	1	1	1
Government			
Regulations	2	3	2
Taxes	2	2	1
Programs	2	2	2
Politics	1	2	2

Table 2.3. Environment factor weights by industry. (cont.)

	Industry Classification		
Factor	Manufacturing	Transportation	Wholesale and Retail Trade
Environment			
Market			
Potential Volume	1	1	1
Proportion	1	1	1
Fertility	1	1	1
Growth	1	1	1
Stability	1	1	2
Outlook	1	1	1
Competition			
Size	1	1	2
Specialization	1	3	2
Entrenchment	1	1	1
Pricing	1	1	2
Counteraction	1	2	1
Suppliers			
Materials	1	2	2
Equipment	1	1	1
Services	1	2	2
Dependency	1	1	1
Government			
Regulations	1	2	1
Taxes	1	2	1
Programs	1	2	1
Politics	1	2	1

Factor	Finance, Insurance, Real Estate	Services	Government
Environment			
Market			
Potential Volume	1	1	2
Proportion	1	1	0
Fertility	1	1	0
Growth	1	1	2
Stability	1	1	0
Outlook	1	1	2
Competition			
Size	1	2	1
Specialization	1	1	1
Entrenchment	1	1	2
Pricing	1	2	1
Counteraction	2	2	3
Suppliers			
Materials	1	1	1
Equipment	1	1	1
Services	1	2	1
Dependency	1	1	1

Table 2-3. Environment factor weights by industry. (cont.)

	Industry Classification		
Factor	Finance, Insurance, Real Estate	Services	Government
Government			
Regulations	2	1	2
Taxes	2	1	3
Programs	1	2	3
Politics	2	2	3

Table 2-4. Venture factor weights by industry.

	Industry Classification		
Factor	Agriculture	Mining	Contract Construction
Venture			
Support			
Chief Executive	1	1	1
Management Group	1	1	1
Trade	1	1	1
Customers	1	1	1
Investment			
Size	1	2	1
Commitment	1	1	1
Maturity Rate	2	2	3
Risk	2	3	2
Return	1	1	1
Salvability	1	2	2
Strategy			
Consistency	1	1	1
Appropriateness	1	1	1
Improvement	1	1	1
Preemption	1	2	2
Necessity	1	1	1
Intuition	1	1	2

Factor	Manufacturing	Transportation	Wholesale and Retail Trade
Venture			
Support			
Chief Executive	1	1	1
Management Group	1	1	1
Trade	1	1	1
Customers	1	1	1
Investment			
Size	1	1	1
Commitment	1	1	1
Maturity Rate	1	1	1
Risk	1	1	1

Table 2-4. Venture factor weights by industry. (cont.)

Industry Classification

Factor	Manufacturing	Transportation	Wholesale and Retail Trade
Return	1	1	1
Salvability	1	1	2
Strategy			
Consistency	1	1	1
Appropriateness	1	1	1
Improvement	1	1	1
Preemption	1	1	1
Necessity	1	2	2
Intuition	1	1	2

Factor	Finance, Insurance, Real Estate	Services	Government
Venture			
Support			
Chief Executive	1	1	3
Management Group	1	1	3
Trade	1	1	2
Customers	1	1	2
Investment			
Size	1	1	1
Commitment	1	1	2
Maturity Rate	1	2	0
Risk	1	2	0
Return	1	1	1
Salvability	1	1	1
Strategy			
Consistency	2	2	2
Appropriateness	2	1	2
Improvement	1	1	3
Preemption	1	2	2
Necessity	2	2	3
Intuition	1	2	2

The basic, unadjusted SAVE analysis assumes that the venturing company is considering a new venture showing few significant operational differences from its existing capabilities—a venture falling into Category A in the displacement matrix. The Category A ventures require no displacement adjustment. However, when substantial differences are expected in the operations required to support a new venture, the relative importance of the major aspects will shift. The *environment* and *venture* aspects will assume greater importance, while the *item* and *company* aspects will decrease in rela-

Table 2-5. Venture displacement classification matrix.

Versatility	Basic Operational Difference			
	Little Difference	Notable Difference	Substantial Difference	Extreme Difference
Good Versatility	A	A	B	C
Limited Versatility	A	B	C	D
Extremely Limited Versatility	A	C	D	E

Weighting factors to be applied to appropriate evaluation factors:

Category A - 1.0
Category B - 2.0
Category C - 3.0
Category D - 4.0
Category E - 5.0

tive importance. Table 2-6 shows the relative importance of the major aspects according to the venture's displacement classification; these weights are based on a manufacturing industry venture, and would vary proportionately in other fields.

Certainty Range Specifications. Technically speaking, certainty range specifications are descriptive refinements rather than adjustments. They provide for telling more about a respondent's judgment about a factor than could be expressed in a single rating number. Instead of simply calling for the respondent's "best judgment" rating, he is asked also to set the upper and lower limits of what he judges to be possible as a rating. For example, if his best judgment rating for a particular factor was "four," he would be asked how high the rating *might* be as a maximum or optimistic limit. Perhaps he would answer, "I *know* it can't be above five." Then, when asked how low he thinks it could be, he might answer, "I don't believe it could possibly be less than two" at the minimum or pessimistic level. The specification of certainty ranges describes a judgment much more clearly and completely than a single pinpoint rating can, and it adds extremely valuable "shading" dimensions to computer processed evaluations, particularly where the program calls for careful construction of the very best composite judgments available.

Judgment Qualifications. As described in the preceding section, a respondent's judgment may extend not only to forming a "best

Table 2-6. Relative importance of major aspects by displacement classification.

Displacement Classification	Percentage Weight by Major Aspect				
	Item	Company	Environment	Venture	Total
A	20.3	29.0	27.5	23.2	100.0
B	17.4	23.4	30.6	28.6	100.0
C	15.6	20.0	33.3	31.1	100.0
D	14.6	18.3	34.2	32.9	100.0
E	13.9	16.9	35.4	33.8	100.0

judgment" rating, but also to the specification of a range of certainty which shows how high or low the "correct" rating might conceivably be. Another dimension which a respondent can describe about his judgment is how well qualified it is. Obviously, a great deal more is known about a respondent's rating of, say, eight on a specific factor, if it is also known whether his answer is based on fact or is simply a wild guess on his part. Table 2-7 describes the various levels of certainty that might be applied to a respondent's ratings, based on his special knowledge of that factor. As shown in the table, the certainty index may range from "wild guess" through "fair estimate" to "known fact."

This kind of judgement description is easily handled in the computer program to color and shade overall venture evaluations, and thereby render interpretations more accurate and meaningful.

Judgment Preference Specifications. Whereas the judgment qualifications provide the respondent or evaluator a means of qualifying his own judgment, the judgment preference specifications provide the chief executive a means of selecting and structuring his organization's best collective judgment on each factor rating. Each evaluator, including the chief executive, members of the management group, and even outside consultants, can be assigned a code identification, so that every rating can be associated with its source. The chief executive can determine exactly how he wants to structure his company's best judgment on any factor of any evaluation by simply expressing his preferences. For example, he might decide to use straight arithmetical averages of all "best judgment" factors qualified as an "educated guess" or better. Or, he may want to

Table 2-7. Certainty index for participants in strategic analysis.

Certainty Index	Level of Certainty
0	Wild Guess
1	Weak Guess
2	Fair Guess
3	Good Guess
4	Educated Guess
5	Fair Estimate
6	Good Estimate
7	Reliable Estimate
8	Accurate Estimate
9	Very Accurate Estimate
10	Known Fact

double or triple the sales manager's rating weights on marketing factors, and increase the technical director's weights on technical factors. Or, he may wish to eliminate the most divergent ratings and average the balance. He may prefer to use weighted averages based on combinations of certainty ranges and judgment qualifications as applied to various individuals' ratings. The important point is to structure the composite ratings to reflect precisely the pattern of judgment which the chief executive believes is best. When the analysis is computerized, these kinds of data are directly convertible by the computer to indicate confidence levels or other measures of rating reliability.

Inclination Adjustments. Any sensitive system based upon subjective judgments must recognize that an individual's ratings tend to reflect his personality to one extent or another. For example, in some evaluations one individual's ratings may average a full point or more above those of anyone else in the group on every factor rated. This simply means that the individual's frames of reference all sit on a higher (or lower) mental plane. He just thinks "eight" where the rest of the group thinks "seven." This is not particularly significant, and it certainly does not indicate a basic deficiency in judgment. But where the tendency can be clearly established as an "inclined pattern," unmistakably habitual in nature, then appropriate adjustments may be introduced for it in order to improve the data and make them more homogeneous.

Special Adjustments. Certain special adjustments may be made at the discretion of the project director when careful study determines that there are unusual considerations present which are not appropriately handled within the framework of factors, weights, and adjustments. The range of special adjustments is normally limited to from zero to two, and in very rare cases it may be extended to three. The purpose of special adjustments is to facilitate recognition and evaluation of exceptional circumstances where the evaluation will clearly benefit by their inclusion. It would make no sense at all to ignore important special factors simply because they are too unusual to be included in the framework of a general evaluation rating system. The greater likelihood of error, however, lies in overvaluation of the unusual conditions. It may well be that what appears to be an important exceptional circumstance is actually covered within one or more factors having general, rather than specific, connotation. It requires substantial experience with SAVE to judge the relative extent to which an unusual condition is actually undervalued in the system. This is the reason why special adjustments are reserved to the discretion of the SAVE project leader.

THE SAVE PROJECT

A SAVE project for a sizable company typically begins with homework by an individual selected to lead the project. This project leader will accumulate the basic profile data from the company's records, along with representative sales literature and other pertinent information. The project leader should receive advance notification of specific venture interests. He will study these materials, familiarize himself with the company's overall situation, identify possible areas of special attention and emphasis, note key questions, and consult with other staff members about the advisability of including additional factors.

Actual evaluation begins with an orientation session, a group presentation and a discussion attended by all of the project's participants.

Next, the chief executive's ranged and qualified ratings are obtained for the best, most representative, and worst items of present output, for past ventures both successful and unsuccessful, and for the proposed ventures. In addition to providing his own ranged and qualified ratings, he should specify his judgment preferences and discuss his ideas about special and venture displacement adjustments, and possible additional factors.

The other project participants' ranged and qualified ratings are next obtained for the best, most representative, and worst items of present output, for past ventures (both successful and unsuccessful), and for the proposed ventures.

All of this information may be computerized, under the direction of the project leader, together with the company's basic profile data. After the data are programmed, processed, tested, cross-correlated, analyzed, and interpreted, they are presented orally and discussed with the rest of the company's management group. Project findings and recommendations are usually prepared in the form of a final written presentation.

The entire project data bank will then be permanently filed in the computer, where it is easily and economically available for updating, revision, reevaluation, and addition at the company's convenience.

A typical SAVE analysis for a small company, or for individuals considering entry or investment in a new business, is far less formal or structured. Adjustments should be kept to an absolute minimum, perhaps involving only the industry adjustment. The evaluator or evaluators will simply go through the 69 factors, summarize the resulting ratings, and critically review any glaring weaknesses. A decision will then be made to go ahead with the project, abandon it, postpone it, study it in greater depth, or attempt to correct the obvious shortcomings before proceeding farther. Regardless of the results or decisions coming from the study, the evaluator or evaluators will have a far better and more thorough understanding of the proposed venture.

3
The Item

The *item* refers to whatever is to be sold. It may range from a single product to a broad line of merchandise, or from a simple mechanical or personal service to an entirely new organization offering a complete range of highly complex professional services.

The item, then, can encompass any new venture, its scope limited only by the venturer's definition.

Every item will fit somewhere within the existing business environment, and will compete with other items within this environment. A new product will compete with existing products serving the same intended functions or markets; a new service will compete with similar services within a market or market area.

Defining what constitutes competitive items—whether products or services—is an important step in the SAVE analysis, and must be done carefully. For example, while "economy" cars may compete in a transportation sense with "luxury" cars, they occupy a certain segment of the total automotive market and would be judged in comparison with other cars in their price class, not with top-of-the-line models. Similarly, the merchandise line carried by a specialty shop would normally be judged relative to other similar specialty shops, and not in comparison with large mass-market merchandisers. The major factor groups in which the item must be rated, relative to directly competitive items, are:

1. Performance,
2. Salability, and
3. Defensibility.

The specific factors incorporated in each of these factor groups are shown in Fig. 3-1. While it is convenient in the following discussions to think of the item as a new product entering an existing market, essentially the same factors will apply to virtually any situation.

PERFORMANCE

Superiority of performance is a salable commodity, whether for a product, a service, or an individual. The item that can consistently and dependably outperform competitive items in its class has an obvious advantage in becoming successful.

Performance may, of necessity, be a function of price, and every product or service will have its own unique set of performance characteristics and criteria. There will be trade-offs (such as luxury vs. economy) in the marketplace, where customers will weigh the desirability of an item against the item's cost.

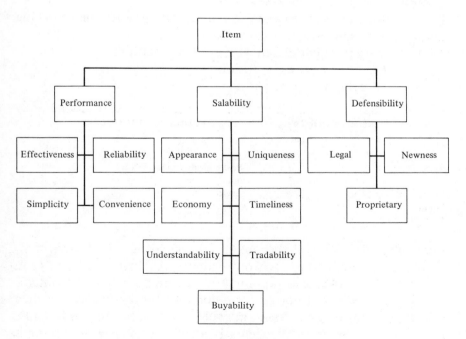

Fig. 3-1. The item model.

The primary determinants of item performance can be grouped into four categories:

1. Effectiveness,
2. Reliability,
3. Simplicity, and
4. Convenience.

In all cases, the primary question to be answered with regard to item performance is, simply:

How well does it work?

Effectiveness. Effectiveness refers to the item's (product or service) ability to produce the desired effect, or to perform its intended function. In assigning a rating to the effectiveness factor, the proposed item must be compared with competitive items in terms of:

How well does it do its intended job?

In rating the item's effectiveness on a scale of 1 to 10, the following guidelines are suggested:

1 = Very poor compared with most competitors.
5 = Meets average competition.
10 = Clearly the industry leader.

Factor Weights by Industry Groups—Effectiveness

Industry Group	Factor Weight	Industry Group	Factor Weight
Agriculture	2	Wholesale and Retail Trade	1
Mining	1	Finance, Insurance, Real Estate	1
Contract Construction	1	Services	1
Manufacturing	1	Government	1
Transportation	1		

Reliability. Reliability is becoming an increasingly important consideration in the buying decision for many products and services in many markets. It is also becoming increasingly difficult to obtain. The product that will not perform consistently, or the service firm that cannot be depended upon, may be common, but they will not be tolerated by customers or clients if a reliable alternative becomes available. Here, the basic question is:

Does the item perform consistently, dependably, and safely?

Reliability ratings can be made on this scale:

1 = Cannot be counted on under all expected conditions.
5 = Meets average competition.
10 = Clearly the industry leader.

Factor Weights by Industry Groups — Reliability

Industry Group	Factor Weight	Industry Group	Factor Weight
Agriculture	1	Wholesale and Retail Trade	2
Mining	3	Finance, Insurance, Real Estate	2
Contract Construction	2	Services	2
Manufacturing	1	Government	2
Transportation	2		

Simplicity. The ultimate goal in design, whether in a product or in an organization, is a simplicity that approaches functional perfection: in other words, the simplest approach that will get the job done. Many good ideas have failed to live up to their initial promise, just because their originators were so overly enthusiastic that they were carried away beyond reason and ended up exaggerating their idea beyond credibility or salability. Complexity for the sake of complexity should be avoided. In rating the proposed item with respect to its simplicity, it is necessary only to ask:

How efficient and uncomplicated is it, compared to competition?

The ratings to be assigned will range from:

1 = Badly over-complicated.
5 = Meets average competition.
10 = Clearly the industry leader.

Factor Weights by Industry Groups — Simplicity

Industry Group	Factor Weight	Industry Group	Factor Weight
Agriculture	1	Wholesale and Retail Trade	1
Mining	1	Finance, Insurance, Real Estate	1
Contract Construction	1	Services	1
Manufacturing	1	Government	1
Transportation	1		

Convenience. Convenience is another factor which has contributed heavily to the success or failure of many new business ventures, particularly in the retail trade area. Convenience might be considered a "non-negative" rather than a "positive" factor, much like the other performance-related factors. In this sense, it might be defined as a "lack or avoidance of inconvenience, or the absence of an unnecessary aggravation." Things that are difficult to install, use, store, repair, get to, or park at will be avoided by many who, but for the inconvenience, might otherwise have become good customers. The proposed item, therefore, should be physically easy to work with, shop at, or otherwise get it to do whatever it is supposed to do. This ease of use or convenience factor will be rated, relative to competition, by answering this question:

Physically, how easy is it to use?

The ratings will be on the following basis:

1 = Very difficult, compared to competition.

5 = Meets average competition.

10 = Clearly the most convenient-to-use item in the industry.

Factor Weights by Industry Groups—Convenience

Industry Group	Factor Weight	Industry Group	Factor Weight
Agriculture	1	Wholesale and Retail Trade	3
Mining	1	Finance, Insurance, Real Estate	2
Contract Construction	1	Services	2
Manufacturing	1	Government	1
Transportation	2		

Summary of Item Performance Factors. The item performance factors can be quickly summarized as follows:

1. *Effectiveness*—does it do its intended job well?
2. *Reliability*—does it perform consistently, dependably, and safely?
3. *Simplicity*—how efficient and uncomplicated is it?
4. *Convenience*—physically, how easy is it to install, use, store, and/or repair?

SALABILITY

Many good products and good ideas have ended up as economic failures, and many mediocre products and ideas have led to outstanding economic results in the marketplace just because of certain defects or advantages related to salability.

The specific reasons that people buy a particular product or choose a particular service are difficult to determine. But whatever they are, the characteristics that make an item salable must be converted into product, service, or item attributes.

The major factors affecting the salability of an item include:

1. Appearance,
2. Uniqueness,
3. Economy,
4. Timeliness,
5. Understandability,
6. Tradability, and
7. Buyability.

The key question to be asked of the item under consideration, with regard to each of these salability factors, is simply:

How well will it sell?

Appearance. Appearance can be an overwhelmingly important factor in some markets and for some products. The appearance appeal may be in the overall decor, layout, and environment of a retail store or professional office, in the aesthetic appeal of an attractive package or a functional-looking piece of machinery, in a distinctive styling that communicates a quality image, or even in the appearance of employees. In some businesses and some products, there is no question that style sells. The question here is:

Is the item to be sold physically and/or functionally attractive?

The rating scale goes like this:

1 = Looks ugly or awkward compared to competition.
5 = Meets average competition.
10 = Clearly the most attractive-appearing item in the industry.

Factor Weights by Industry Groups — Appearance

Industry Group	Factor Weight	Industry Group	Factor Weight
Agriculture	1	Wholesale and Retail Trade	1
Mining	1	Finance, Insurance, Real Estate	1
Contract Construction	1	Services	1
Manufacturing	1	Government	2
Transportation	2		

Uniqueness. A product or service that offers certain unique or distinguishing characteristics when compared with competing products or services is certain to have some advantages in terms of marketability. One of the basic principles of salesmanship is, in fact, the USP—the *unique selling proposition*—which emphasizes the salable points that set the product or service being sold apart from its competition. In determining uniqueness, the question to be asked is:

Does the item being sold have any important exclusive features and talking points capable of supporting strong promotion?

The ratings are:

1 = No exclusive features.

5 = On balance, exclusive features merely offset those of competitive items.

10 = Very important and easily appreciated exclusive features.

Factor Weights by Industry Groups — Uniqueness

Industry Group	Factor Weight	Industry Group	Factor Weight
Agriculture	1	Wholesale and Retail Trade	1
Mining	1	Finance, Insurance, Real Estate	1
Contract Construction	1	Services	1
Manufacturing	1	Government	1
Transportation	2		

Economy. Money is valuable, and every business must face up to economic realities. What is often required is not the best possible product or service, but the cheapest that will work. Obviously, a knowledge of both the market and the competition is essential in determining the appropriate trade-offs. There is perhaps no single greater competitive advantage than a lower price than competitors. It should also be recognized that customers or clients may lack sophistication in their economic evaluations of a prospective product or service. They may not conduct or even understand a discounted cash flow analysis showing the benefits of greater future savings resulting from a higher initial investment, and the present value of future cash flows may hold little significance to the prospective buyer. A high price is seldom a salable advantage. Consequently, the question to be answered in this respect is:

How does this item's cost compare with competition?

The rating scale for the economy factor is:

 1 = Costs more than competitive items to buy, install, use, and/or maintain.
 5 = Meets average competition over reasonable life span.
10 = Offers substantial relative savings, both in first cost and in subsequent use.

Factor Weights by Industry Groups — Economy			
Industry Group	Factor Weight	Industry Group	Factor Weight
Agriculture	2	Wholesale and Retail Trade	1
Mining	1	Finance, Insurance, Real Estate	1
Contract Construction	1	Services	1
Manufacturing	1	Government	1
Transportation	2		

Timeliness. There is a season for all things, and proper timing can contribute much to the success of a new product, service, or other business venture. Successful mass merchandisers, for example, have long recognized and capitalized on their knowledge of consumers' seasonal buying habits in planning their advertising, promotional, inventory, cash flow, and personnel requirements. In hunting ducks, it is necessary to shoot the ducks when they are flying, not necessarily when it is preferred by or convenient to the duck hunter. New products or services are timely only when there is a market awaiting them. What determines timeliness may be the season, the location, the economy, the cash position of the venturer, or any number of other factors. It is important to determine exactly what constitutes timeliness for the particular venture being considered. The question is:

Is this an opportune time for the proposed venture?

The timeliness ratings are:

  1 = Present timing is clearly unfavorable.

  5 = Present timing is neither favorable nor unfavorable.

10 = Present timing is very advantageous.

Factor Weights by Industry Groups—Timeliness			
Industry Group	Factor Weight	Industry Group	Factor Weight
Agriculture	3	Wholesale and Retail Trade	1
Mining	1	Finance, Insurance, Real Estate	1
Contract Construction	2	Services	2
Manufacturing	1	Government	2
Transportation	2		

Understandability. Customers tend to distrust things they cannot or do not understand, and any product, service, or business that requires a lengthy explanation is suffering a distinct competitive disadvantage. Whether the item is a product that requires major training or retraining of personnel, or a service offering benefits that are difficult to define, measure, or understand, the problem is apparent: without a clear understanding of the item and its benefits, the customer or client will not have a clear understanding of its true value to him. The question to be asked of the item is therefore:

Can its functions and merits be easily and quickly understood by potential users?

The ratings are:

  1 = Requires a great deal of explanation or re-education to get the story across.

  5 = Meets average competition in ease of comprehension.

10 = Far easier to understand and appreciate than present competition.

Factor Weights by Industry Groups—Understandability			
Industry Group	Factor Weight	Industry Group	Factor Weight
Agriculture	1	Wholesale and Retail Trade	2
Mining	1	Finance, Insurance, Real Estate	1
Contract Construction	1	Services	2
Manufacturing	1	Government	1
Transportation	2		

Tradability. While uniqueness of a product or service is an important selling point, being too unique or unusual may cause problems in a market that has become accustomed to more common or traditional items. Acceptability of a new item to the trade, as opposed to acceptance to ultimate consumers of the item, is essential in achieving the necessary distribution. The question to be asked of a proposed product, service, or venture is:

How well adapted to the proposed trade is the item?

The rating scale is:

  1 = Requires special attention and handling that is apt to be resented by salesmen, jobbers, distributors, suppliers, dealers, users, and so forth.

  5 = Meets average competition.

  10 = Trade views it as significantly better adapted to their operations than competitive items.

Factor Weights by Industry Groups—Tradability

Industry Group	Factor Weight	Industry Group	Factor Weight
Agriculture	2	Wholesale and Retail Trade	3
Mining	1	Finance, Insurance, Real Estate	1
Contract Construction	2	Services	2
Manufacturing	1	Government	2
Transportation	1		

Buyability. The buyability or availability of a product, service, or other item to its potential customers is critical. Many customers will not go out of their way to obtain even an obviously superior item; they instead prefer the convenience of being able to buy and have the item serviced at the least inconvenient location. Buyability, then, is another "non-negative" item attribute—people will not buy something that is difficult to buy because of its lack of availability at the point of sale. They will, given the choice between a preferred item that is not readily available and a less preferred item that is easily available, often choose the less preferred (but available) item. The buyability factor is important in all types of businesses, particularly those dealing directly with the public. The primary question regarding an item's buyability is:

To what extent does the buyer feel a conscious need for the item when encountered at the point of sale?

The ratings relating to item buyability are:

1 = The item is not available at the point of sale and the buying urge is only casual at best.

5 = The item is generally available and the buying urge normal at the point of sale.

10 = The buying urge is irresistible at the point of sale.

Factor Weights by Industry Groups — Buyability			
Industry Group	Factor Weight	Industry Group	Factor Weight
Agriculture	1	Wholesale and Retail Trade	2
Mining	1	Finance, Insurance, Real Estate	2
Contract Construction	1	Services	2
Manufacturing	1	Government	1
Transportation	1		

Summary of Salability Factors. The seven factors relating to the salability of a proposed new item are:

1. *Appearance*—is it physically and/or functionally attractive?
2. *Uniqueness*—does it have important exclusive features and talking points capable of supporting strong promotion?
3. *Economy*—how does its cost compare with competition?
4. *Timeliness*—is this an opportune time for it?
5. *Understandability*—can its functions and merits be easily and quickly understood by users?
6. *Tradability*—how well adapted to the proposed trade is it?
7. *Buyability*—to what extent does the buyer feel a conscious need for the item when encountered at the point of sale?

DEFENSIBILITY

Any new venture that cannot be defended against its direct competition in order to maintain its exclusivity is in a weak position, at the mercy of its existing and potential competitors. The type of protection needed by a new venture depends upon the nature of the venture itself. A new product may need legal protection in the form of patents, while a new retail store may need some assurance that competitors will not dilute its market by moving nearby or even into the same trade area.

Such protection is difficult to obtain, since there is little that any new business can do about an imaginative competitor, except to be even more imaginative. Successful products are quickly duplicated, and successful businesses are quickly imitated. This brings to mind the following passage from Rudyard Kipling's poem, *The Mary Gloster*, where the firm's founder is explaining to his son why he was more successful than his many competitors:

> *They copied all they could follow,*
> *but they couldn't copy my mind,*
> *And I left 'em sweating and stealing*
> *a year and a half behind.*

There is no such thing as a completely defensible business position; the only real defense is the ability to move and stay ahead of the competition. Legal and proprietary rights regarding new ventures can only delay the competition briefly, giving the venturer a little head start. A head start, though, may be the only advantage needed; in business, as in sports, it is easier to stay ahead than it is to come from behind.

The defensibility of an item can be measured in terms of three factors:

1. Legal,
2. Newness, and
3. Proprietary.

Legal. Some of the legal means by which a business venture can be protected from competition include patents, trademarks, copyrights, licenses, and franchises. A *patent* is an exclusionary right to prevent others from using the idea or invention claimed by the patent, whether or not the patent owner intends to use it himself. *Trademarks* include words, names, symbols, or combinations of these devices that are used to identify the goods or products being sold or advertised under that trademark. *Copyrights* are intended to prevent the unauthorized use or copying of original "creative" works, including writing, art, photographs, music, and so forth. *Licenses* may be granted by the owners of legally protected items to allow their use on some prescribed basis, ranging from exclusive to local. *Franchises* operate on much the same basis, with the holder granted certain rights to use whatever item is being franchised by the franchise owner. In assessing the legal defensibility of an item, this question should be asked:

How firmly are the item's important features protected by patents, copyrights, trademarks, licenses, franchises, or other legal means?

The rating scale for the item's legal defensibility is

1 = No formal protection where it would be desirable.

5 = Significant protection seems assured for at least a moderate period of time (five years or so).

10 = Significant basic protection seems assured for a considerable length of time (ten years or more).

Factor Weights by Industry Groups — Legal

Industry Group	Factor Weight	Industry Group	Factor Weight
Agriculture	1	Wholesale and Retail Trade	2
Mining	3	Finance, Insurance, Real Estate	1
Contract Construction	1	Services	1
Manufacturing	1	Government	2
Transportation	3		

Newness. The first product or service on the market has the jump on its competition, although it has also incurred the development expenses and initial promotional costs associated with being the leader. Hopefully, the competitive advantages gained by being first can be maintained at least long enough to cover the economic disadvantages, and the new item will become firmly entrenched in the marketplace before competing items can be brought to market. The simpler the item—and consequently, the easier and quicker to imitate—the faster it must be exploited. The question is:

Does the new item have much of a jump on competition from the standpoint of development time?

The rating scale is:

1 = It is a conventional item in a mature industry.

5 = It is a new concept in a mature industry.

10 = It is a new concept in a young industry, thus requiring a long lead time.

Factor Weights by Industry Groups — Newness

Industry Group	Factor Weight	Industry Group	Factor Weight
Agriculture	1	Wholesale and Retail Trade	1
Mining	2	Finance, Insurance, Real Estate	1
Contract Construction	1	Services	1
Manufacturing	1	Government	1
Transportation	2		

Proprietary. Some products and services may offer means for defense from competition by factors other than their legality and newness. A business's new venture may be, for example, protected by captive sources of supply or captive sales (such as to franchisees), or the firm may have access to special know-how or trade secrets unavailable to competitive firms, or it may be able to support the new venture with a strong line of companion items or services. While trade or process secrets may not be patentable, knowing almost anything that is not known to competitors can result in a real competitive advantage. In addition to secrets of a technological nature, important proprietary advantages may be found in business information and customer lists. The question is:

Does the proposed item enjoy special proprietary advantages over its competitors?

The ratings for this factor are:

1 = Major competitors have substantial net advantages in this respect.

5 = On balance, its situation meets average competition.

10 = It has enormous special advantages of this kind.

Factor Weights by Industry Groups — Proprietary

Industry Group	Factor Weight	Industry Group	Factor Weight
Agriculture	2	Wholesale and Retail Trade	2
Mining	2	Finance, Insurance, Real Estate	2
Contract Construction	1	Services	2
Manufacturing	1	Government	1
Transportation	1		

Summary of Defensibility Factors. The three major factors measuring the extent to which the exclusivity of the proposed item can be maintained and defended against direct competition are:

1. *Legal*—how firmly are its important features protected by patents, copyrights, trademarks, licenses, titles, or franchises?
2. *Newness*—does it have much of a jump on competition from the standpoint of development time?
3. *Proprietary*—does it enjoy special advantages such as captive supplies, captive sales, process secrets, brand preference, or a strong line of companion items?

SUMMARY OF ITEM FACTORS

Evaluation of the item's competitive effectiveness is measured in terms of 14 specific factors, divided into three major factor groups. To determine how good an item is, compared with competitive items, requires thorough answers to these basic questions:

1. *Performance.* How well does the proposed item work, when compared with competitive items in terms of effectiveness, reliability, simplicity, and convenience?
2. *Salability.* How well will it sell, when measured against its competition with respect to its appearance, uniqueness, economy, timeliness, understandability, tradability, and buyability?
3. *Defensibility.* To what extent can the company maintain its exclusivity and defend the proposed item or venture against direct competition, whether by its newness, or legal or proprietary means?

A SAVE rating sheet for the analysis of item factors is shown in Fig. 3-2.

In using the SAVE rating sheet, the rating determined for each of the 14 factors is entered in the first column. The weighting factor for the industry group in which the new venture falls goes in the second column, and the factor score is the product of the first two columns. The score thus derived may range from one (a factor rating of one and a factor weight of one) up to a maximum of 30 (a factor rating of ten and a factor weight of three).

Factor	Factor Rating	Factor Weight	Factor Score	Factor Group	Factor Group Score
Effectiveness	____	____	____		
Reliability	____	____	____	} Performance	____
Simplicity	____	____	____		
Convenience	____	____	____		
Appearance	____	____	____		
Uniqueness	____	____	____		
Economy	____	____	____	} Salability	____
Timeliness	____	____	____		
Understandability	____	____	____		
Tradability	____	____	____		
Buyability	____	____	____		
Legal	____	____	____	} Defensibility	____
Newness	____	____	____		
Proprietary	____	____	____		
Total Item Score					____
Total Score Possible					____
Item Efficiency Percentage					____

Fig. 3-2. SAVE rating sheet for item factors.

The factor scores are then combined by factor groups, giving factor group scores, and the factor group scores are totaled to give a total item score.

The maximum item score possible is ten times the total of all 14 factor weights; this total varies by industry groups, as follows.

Maximum Possible Score

Industry Group	Performance	Salability	Defensibility	Total
Agriculture	50	110	40	200
Mining	60	70	70	200
Contract Construction	50	90	30	170
Manufacturing	40	70	30	140
Transportation	60	120	60	240
Wholesale and Retail Trade	70	110	50	230
Finance, Insurance, Real Estate	60	80	40	180
Services	60	110	40	210
Government	50	100	40	190

Finally, the total item score is divided by the maximum possible score to determine the item efficiency percentage. This efficiency percentage represents the item's "grade" in a competitive sense. A score of 80 percent or better is exceptional, reflecting few weaknesses of any significance. Any score under 60 percent should be viewed with the thought of strengthening the deficient areas before making any further commitments.

4
The Company

The capabilities—or lack of capabilities—of the company or organization entering a new business venture are among the most important factors in terms of the venture's success potential. In several industry groups (mining, manufacturing, wholesale and retail trade, and service businesses), the company's characteristics and capabilities are *the* most important of the four major aspects governing venture success.

For ventures involving extreme operational differences from the existing business, the company's characteristics become relatively less important; such extreme differences mean simply that the company's present resources and strengths cannot be utilized in the new venture anyway, and the necessary capabilities will have to be developed or acquired.

The three major groups of factors relating to the company's or organization's capabilities involve:

1. Marketing,
2. Technology, and
3. Production.

Of these three factor groups, marketing is generally the most important and least easily acquired capability. Figure 4-1 shows the 20 factors associated with the three factor groups.

MARKETING

In most industries, a company's marketing capability is the single

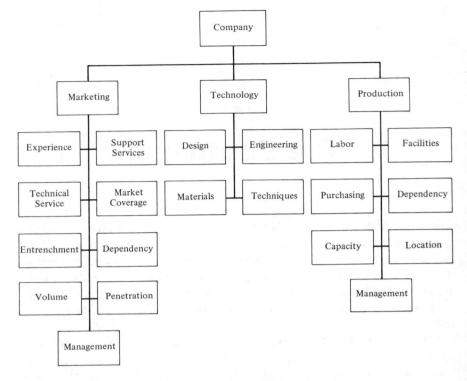

Fig. 4-1. The company model.

most important factor contributing to the success of a new venture. In just a few industry groups, the firm's marketing abilities are exceeded in importance only by the item's salability factors.

Marketing encompasses far more than the basically simple process of moving a finished product to an eager consumer. A complex economy requires a similarly complex marketing system. Some 97 percent of all product sales, for example, require the participation of two or more firms, with every firm in the distribution chain dependent to some extent on other firms in the chain.

In moving a product from its producer or manufacturer to its ultimate consumer, two basic flows are involved: (1) the physical movement of the product from its origin to its point of consumption and (2) the two-way flow of information that precedes, accompanies, and follows the product's physical movement. The information flow encompasses the product planning, purchasing, promotion, and selling. The efficiency of the distribution channel depends on how well these flows are administered.

There are also several different strategic approaches to marketing a new product or a new business. These can be grouped into three categories:

1. Identify what the market wants, then attempt to supply these wants.
2. Decide what is to be sold, then attempt to find the appropriate market for the goods or services.
3. Attempt to create a market demand for whatever is to be offered.

The first approach is market-oriented, the second, product-oriented, and the third, marketing-oriented. They might also be described as developing new products that can be offered to existing customers, developing new customers for existing markets, or introducing new products to new customers.

The company's or organization's marketing capabilities are measured in terms of the following nine factors:

1. Experience,
2. Support services,
3. Technical service,
4. Market coverage,
5. Entrenchment,
6. Dependency,
7. Volume,
8. Penetration, and
9. Management.

The main thrust of these nine marketing factors is to determine:

How much does the company have of what it takes to market the item effectively?

Experience. "Experience is a difficult teacher; she gives the test first, and the lesson afterward." This statement is nowhere more appropriate than with marketing. So little is actually known in marketing that much must be learned through experimentation. Even experience acquired in closely related lines may not carry over directly into the new venture. Promotion, merchandising, and advertising all require different approaches for different ventures, and the best approach may be unpredictable in advance. The important question regarding the company's marketing experience is:

> *How well does the company know the market and understand how to reach, sell, and service the market?*

The answers are rated as follows:

1 = The company has severe disadvantages in this respect, compared to competitors.

5 = The company is equal to the average competition.

10 = The company has extremely important competitive advantages in savvy and actual experience in this phase of marketing.

Factor Weights by Industry Groups — Experience

Industry Group	Factor Weight	Industry Group	Factor Weight
Agriculture	1	Wholesale and Retail Trade	2
Mining	1	Finance, Insurance, Real Estate	1
Contract Construction	1	Services	2
Manufacturing	1	Government	2
Transportation	1		

Support Services. Support services refer primarily to the flow of information through marketing channels. The efficiency of the distribution channel depends largely upon how well the support services are handled. The typical support services for a manufactured product, for example, include order handling, warehousing, delivery time, freight expense, warranties, complaint adjustments, and sales analysis. Other industries will find other support service factors to be more appropriate. In each case, though, the question will be:

> *How does the company compare with its competition with respect to the support services appropriate to the particular line of business being considered?*

The rating scale goes like this:

1 = Company has severe disadvantages compared with competition.

5 = Company generally meets average competition.

10 = Company is clearly the industry leader in all important categories.

Factor Weights by Industry Groups — Support Services

Industry Group	Factor Weight	Industry Group	Factor Weight
Agriculture	1	Wholesale and Retail Trade	1
Mining	1	Finance, Insurance, Real Estate	1
Contract Construction	1	Services	1
Manufacturing	1	Government	1
Transportation	1		

Technical Service. The availability of adequate, convenient, and economical technical support services may be a major consideration in selecting one product or service over another, both in industrial and consumer markets. The company must determine the amount, type, and value of services to be offered. Depending on the specific nature of the venture, it is necessary to be competitive in terms of application, installation, or assembly instructions, user instructions, test and competitive comparison data, technical sales correspondence, technical sales training, and inclusion in standard industry specification data. In rating the company's technical service capabilities, the following question is appropriate:

How does the company compare with its average competition in terms of technical sales support?

The ratings are:

1 = Seriously deficient compared with competition.

5 = Generally equals average competition.

10 = Clearly the industry leader in providing technical data regarding materials, usage and installation information, test results, and so forth.

Factor Weights by Industry Groups — Technical Service

Industry Group	Factor Weight	Industry Group	Factor Weight
Agriculture	1	Wholesale and Retail Trade	1
Mining	1	Finance, Insurance, Real Estate	1
Contract Construction	1	Services	1
Manufacturing	1	Government	1
Transportation	1		

Market Coverage. Many good products and services have gone unsold simply because the company failed to cover its markets adequately. If the appropriate market for an item is undetected, there is no way to bring the product or service and its potential consumers together. To be effective, the national market should be well covered in terms of associated items, major market salaried representatives, active representation throughout the geographic market area, advertising, standard references, sales training, territory intelligence, and market research. This all leads into the question:

How completely does the company presently cover the market?

The ratings for the answer are:

1 = Company has no significant coverage in this field.

5 = Company has some representation in all major markets.

10 = Company has good representation throughout the entire national or geographic market.

Factor Weights by Industry Groups — Market Coverage			
Industry Group	Factor Weight	Industry Group	Factor Weight
Agriculture	1	Wholesale and Retail Trade	1
Mining	1	Finance, Insurance, Real Estate	1
Contract Construction	1	Services	1
Manufacturing	1	Government	1
Transportation	1		

Entrenchment. Entrenchment is a measure of the market's loyalty to the company in the field being served or considered. It is an easy factor to overestimate, since there is very little product or company loyalty that cannot be overcome by a price just a few dollars lower. Nevertheless, the entrenchment of a company in the marketplace is one of the most important factors affecting the success of a new product or service in that field, since some special effort is always required to win a customer away from his existing supplier. The importance of developing a strong loyalty in both typical and key customers, therefore, cannot be overemphasized. The question is:

How strong is the company's present trade and customer loyalty in this field?

The answers are rated as follows:

1 = Company has no present distribution, dealers, or customers here, and consequently no consumer loyalty.

5 = Company has many loyal distributors and dealers, but would require nearly all new customers.

10 = Company has present trade, present customers, and excellent loyalty.

Factor Weights by Industry Groups — Entrenchment

Industry Group	Factor Weight	Industry Group	Factor Weight
Agriculture	1	Wholesale and Retail Trade	2
Mining	1	Finance, Insurance, Real Estate	2
Contract Construction	3	Services	3
Manufacturing	1	Government	3
Transportation	2		

Dependency. A company whose market is dependent upon just a few major accounts is in a particularly vulnerable position should one or more of these key accounts be lost. Many examples could be cited regarding companies whose entire financial situation depended upon just a single product for a single customer. Then, when the relationship is suddenly, sometimes surprisingly, terminated, the supplier is left with unsalable inventory, unusable resources, and unpayable bills, along with a real problem in trying to develop new markets, customers, or capabilities to stay afloat. The dependency of the company on individual accounts, individual representatives, trades preoccupied with other matters, dealers preoccupied with other lines, or salesmen preoccupied with other items should be carefully questioned:

To what extent does the company's applicable marketing strength depend upon just a few individuals or accounts?

Ratings for the dependency factor are:

1 = Entirely dependent on one person or account.

5 = A fair distribution of dependencies at most levels.

10 = No individual or account represents more than 5 percent or so of associated sales.

Factor Weights by Industry Groups — Dependency

Industry Group	Factor Weight	Industry Group	Factor Weight
Agriculture	1	Wholesale and Retail Trade	1
Mining	1	Finance, Insurance, Real Estate	1
Contract Construction	1	Services	1
Manufacturing	1	Government	1
Transportation	1		

Volume. Whenever a new product or a new venture is introduced, the introduction can be made most effectively if it fits in easily and compatibly with the company's other products or ventures; the greater the company's volume in related items, the greater the chances of success for the new item. Also, the company's degree of specialization in related items is important. If a substantial portion of the company's total sales volume is in related lines, the new line's potential is greatly enhanced. The key question here is:

What was the company's volume in associated items last year?

The rating scale is:

  1 = Less than 5 percent of total company sales.

  5 = About 20 percent of total company sales.

10 = 60 percent or more of total company sales.

Factor Weights by Industry Groups — Volume

Industry Group	Factor Weight	Industry Group	Factor Weight
Agriculture	1	Wholesale and Retail Trade	1
Mining	1	Finance, Insurance, Real Estate	1
Contract Construction	1	Services	1
Manufacturing	1	Government	1
Transportation	1		

Penetration. A company having a substantial share of the market for items related to the proposed new item greatly increases its chances for success. Market penetration is closely related to the preceding factor, market volume, but adds another dimension: the total market for related items. In assessing the company's competitive position with respect to its market penetration, the following question should be asked:

What is the company's share of the total market for associated items?

The answers rate as follows:

1 = Company has no really associative items at present.
5 = Approximately 5 percent and stable.
10 = Over 10 percent and increasing.

Factor Weights by Industry Groups — Penetration

Industry Group	Factor Weight	Industry Group	Factor Weight
Agriculture	1	Wholesale and Retail Trade	1
Mining	1	Finance, Insurance, Real Estate	1
Contract Construction	1	Services	1
Manufacturing	1	Government	2
Transportation	1		

Management. Marketing or sales management is obviously a key factor in the company's efforts to promote a new venture of any type. Marketing management must be able to recognize and analyze market data in order to understand the complex workings of the marketplace, so that appropriate plans can be made for the future. The marketing manager's scope, then, spans the past, present, and future, and involves analysis, control, and planning. It should also be noted that a high sales volume is not necessarily indicative of good sales management, and that poor management on the part of competitors is not necessarily an advantage. Poor management often results in the "bad driving out the good," particularly where the bad management shows up in unwarranted or unrealistic price cutting or sales policies. The question here is:

Is the company well situated for this item in terms of sales management?

The answers to this question are rated as follows:

1 = Weak capability; no similar experience.
5 = Good capability; substantial experience in managing sales of dissimilar items.
10 = Excellent capability; long and successful experience in managing sales of similar items.

Factor Weights by Industry Groups — Management

Industry Group	Factor Weight	Industry Group	Factor Weight
Agriculture	1	Wholesale and Retail Trade	1
Mining	1	Finance, Insurance, Real Estate	2
Contract Construction	1	Services	2
Manufacturing	1	Government	1
Transportation	1		

Summary of Marketing Factors. The nine marketing factors, which together constitute the most important single factor group, can be summarized with the following questions:

1. *Experience*—how well does the company know the market and understand how to reach, sell, and service the market?
2. *Support Services*—how does the company compare with its competition with respect to the support services appropriate to the particular line of business being considered?
3. *Technical Service*—how does the company compare with its average competition in terms of technical sales support?
4. *Market Coverage*—how completely does the company presently cover the market?
5. *Entrenchment*—how strong is the company's present trade and customer loyalty in this field?
6. *Dependency*—to what extent does the company's applicable marketing strength depend upon just a few individuals or accounts?
7. *Volume*—what was the company's volume in associated items last year?
8. *Penetration*—what is the company's share of the total market for associated items?
9. *Management*—is the company well situated for this item in terms of sales management?

TECHNOLOGY

A certain amount of technical know-how is required for success in virtually every business. Even in nontechnology businesses, technology has a significant impact. Many of the complex problems confronting a company's management can be solved only by taking into account a combination of technical, economic, managerial, political, and social considerations.

Technology provides the basis for every industry, and management must stay abreast of the new technological developments in order to keep up with competition. The huge quantities of information generated in all businesses is in itself a technological problem and requires technological solutions. Even the small retail or service shop is at a competitive disadvantage if it is unable to apply the latest technology in sales analysis, inventory planning, financial control, and cash flow forecasting.

The factors included in the technology category are:

1. Design,
2. Engineering,
3. Materials, and
4. Techniques.

These factors carry different meanings in the different industry groups. The term *engineering*, for example, may refer specifically to the work performed by licensed professional engineers in some fields, or simply to the company's ability to solve or manage its business problems. Similarly, *design* may involve the design of complex industrial machinery or the layout of a retail store's interior, while *techniques* refer generally to the means by which the company handles its normal day-to-day operations.

Design. In a technological sense, *design* refers to the creative aspects and concepts of a new project. In a business sense, *design* can be interpreted as planning (or designing) a course of action to meet future needs. The important question to be asked is:

How does the company compare with competition in terms of its design (or planning) competence?

The replies to this question are rated:

1 = Company has no in-house design or planning experience of the types required in this venture.

5 = Company can consistently match competition's design and/or planning competence.

10 = Company fairly expects to maintain competitive superiority in all phases of design and/or planning competence.

Factor Weights by Industry Groups — Design			
Industry Group	Factor Weight	Industry Group	Factor Weight
Agriculture	1	Wholesale and Retail Trade	1
Mining	1	Finance, Insurance, Real Estate	1
Contract Construction	1	Services	1
Manufacturing	1	Government	1
Transportation	1		

Engineering. Like design, engineering can be interpreted differently. In its technological sense, engineering is defined as the application of technological principles in solving mechanical problems. In nontechnical businesses, engineering is more appropriately defined as the management of business problems. Either way, engineering can be considered a problem-solving discipline, and the capabilities of a company to solve its problems—whether of a technical, economic, social, or other nature—are important for the company's success. The appropriate question is:

How does the company compare with competition in terms of its engineering (problem-solving) capability?

The answers are rated as follows:

1 = No in-house engineering (problem-solving) experience or capability of the types required.

5 = On balance, company is equal to competition.

10 = Company has the best engineering (problem-solving) know-how in the industry.

Factor Weights by Industry Groups — Engineering			
Industry Group	Factor Weight	Industry Group	Factor Weight
Agriculture	1	Wholesale and Retail Trade	1
Mining	2	Finance, Insurance, Real Estate	1
Contract Construction	1	Services	1
Manufacturing	1	Government	1
Transportation	1		

Materials. A thorough knowledge of the materials involved in the proposed item is a valuable asset, whether the item is a complex piece of industrial machinery, a mineral ore or agricultural product, or an article of wearing apparel. Materials knowledge in some industries carries a highly technical connotation, while in other industries the materials knowledge may be more concerned with the marketability of the item being sold. Either way, the important question concerns whether or not the company has the appropriate type of materials knowledge:

> *How well does the company know the materials involved in this item?*

Answers are rated this way:

  1 = The materials technology is completely foreign.
  5 = On balance, materials technology equals competition.
10 = Company has well-recognized leadership in materials technology.

Factor Weights by Industry Groups — Materials

Industry Group	Factor Weight	Industry Group	Factor Weight
Agriculture	2	Wholesale and Retail Trade	1
Mining	3	Finance, Insurance, Real Estate	1
Contract Construction	1	Services	1
Manufacturing	1	Government	1
Transportation	1		

Techniques. Techniques refer to the methods used to get things done in the regular course of business. Some businesses are extremely technique-oriented. In agriculture, mining, and construction, for example, the company's know-how of industry techniques constitutes the single most important factor in the success of a new venture. The pertinent question, regardless of the industry in which the company operates or in which the new venture falls, is:

> *How competitive is the company in terms of methods, systems, and process techniques?*

The following rating scale is employed:

  1 = Not knowledgeable.

5 = Equal to average competition.
10 = Clearly the industry leader.

Factor Weights by Industry Groups—Techniques

Industry Group	Factor Weight	Industry Group	Factor Weight
Agriculture	3	Wholesale and Retail Trade	1
Mining	3	Finance, Insurance, Real Estate	1
Contract Construction	3	Services	2
Manufacturing	1	Government	2
Transportation	2		

Summary of Technology Factors. Technological know-how in four main areas defines the company's competency in this factor group. The four factors are:

1. *Design*—how does the company compare with competition in terms of its design (or planning) competence?
2. *Engineering*—how does the company compare with competition in terms of its engineering (problem-solving) capability?
3. *Materials*—how well does the company know the materials involved in this item?
4. *Techniques*—how competitive is the company in terms of methods, systems, and process techniques?

PRODUCTION

The company must be able to produce, provide, or in some cases, acquire, its products or services competitively. Production can be defined here as any process or procedure used to create the goods or services having utility or value. The production process involves the coordination and utilization of physical, human, and economic factors, such as the *4 Ms* in construction—men, machines, materials, and money.

Every production process has three distinct components: (1) the inputs, (2) the process, and (3) the outputs. The inputs in the production process may include labor, materials, energy, money, and/or other resources. The process involves the conversion of these resources into the ultimate goods or services to be offered or sold—the outputs.

Seven factors are considered in assessing the company's overall production capabilities:

1. Labor,
2. Facilities,
3. Purchasing,
4. Dependency,
5. Capacity,
6. Location, and
7. Management.

The production function, by means of these seven factors, measures how well the company can convert its resources into salable items.

Labor. A company's employees rank among its most important assets. Whether ranking as unskilled labor or as highly trained professionals, labor is an essential part of the production process that provides the company's output. Some of the points to consider in assessing a company's labor situation include employee attitudes, union attitudes, job classification flexibility, key production skills, key maintenance skills, direct labor hourly rates, and fringe benefits and costs. In view of these considerations, the question is:

How does the company's present labor situation compare with competitors?

Answers rank as follows:
 1 = No experience in key skills; relatively high labor rates.
 5 = Skills are equal to average competition.
10 = Company's labor superiority is a clear-cut competitive advantage.

Factor Weights by Industry Groups — Labor

Industry Group	Factor Weight	Industry Group	Factor Weight
Agriculture	1	Wholesale and Retail Trade	1
Mining	1	Finance, Insurance, Real Estate	1
Contract Construction	1	Services	2
Manufacturing	1	Government	1
Transportation	1		

Facilities. Facilities refer to the physical resources that provide for or contribute to the ease of production. As such, facilities include buildings, machinery, equipment, furniture, fixtures, and related items aiding in the conversion of resource inputs into marketable outputs. Some of the major considerations include plant efficiency, equipment, automation, testing and experimentation, storage, attractiveness, and flexibility of the existing facilities. The important point is that the company's facilities be adequate to perform the necessary functions in whatever field the venture involves, and that they are at least competitive with the facilities of others in the same business. Ask:

How do the company's facilities compare with competition?

The rating scale is:

  1 = Serious net disadvantage compared with competition.
  5 = Equal to average competition.
 10 = Company's facilities are far superior to competition.

Factor Weights by Industry Groups — Facilities

Industry Group	Factor Weight	Industry Group	Factor Weight
Agriculture	1	Wholesale and Retail Trade	1
Mining	2	Finance, Insurance, Real Estate	1
Contract Construction	1	Services	1
Manufacturing	1	Government	1
Transportation	1		

Purchasing. Purchasing is one of the first of the important operations of any business, and skillful buying is essential for profitable operations. Purchasing involves the details of deciding on the sources of supply, the optimum timing for these purchases, and the quantities to be ordered at any one time. Close attention must be paid to salesmen, trade journals, catalogs, and the specific likes and dislikes of present and prospective clients and customers. Some of the major considerations in evaluating a company's purchasing activities include the availability and price of raw materials, components, equipment, supplies, transportation, utilities, and production services. Good purchasing is a combination of science and art, requiring careful analysis, good communications, and good judgment. The key question is:

How does the company's purchasing situation stack up against competition?

The answers rate as follows:

1 = The company has very substantial competitive disadvantages in purchasing.

5 = On balance, the company's situation is about equal to competition.

10 = The company possesses a huge competitive advantage in its purchasing.

Factor Weights by Industry Groups—Purchasing			
Industry Group	Factor Weight	Industry Group	Factor Weight
Agriculture	2	Wholesale and Retail Trade	2
Mining	2	Finance, Insurance, Real Estate	1
Contract Construction	1	Services	1
Manufacturing	1	Government	1
Transportation	1		

Dependency. Overdependency on others for production capabilities, materials, or supplies poses as serious a problem as overdependency in the company's marketing program. Should anything go wrong in any number of factors, production problems can result. Consequently, the company's vulnerability to potential production problem areas such as technical production know-how, key skills, union harmony, supervision, raw materials and components, equipment and supplies, suppliers, and contracted services, should be assessed. For the proposed item, ask this question:

To what extent is the company's production capability vulnerable in terms of overdependency?

Ratings are assigned as follows:

1 = Very uncomfortable degree of dependence upon one person or factor.

5 = Replacements are probably available quickly and locally.

10 = Replacements are definitely available within the company.

Factor Weights by Industry Groups — Dependency

Industry Group	Factor Weight	Industry Group	Factor Weight
Agriculture	1	Wholesale and Retail Trade	1
Mining	1	Finance, Insurance, Real Estate	1
Contract Construction	1	Services	1
Manufacturing	1	Government	1
Transportation	1		

Capacity. Most operations (manufacturing, retail, service, or other) operate most efficiently, effectively, and economically as their productive output approaches their productive capacity. In looking at a new venture, it should be recognized that, while it is important to have sufficient capacity to produce the new item, it is also important from an economic standpoint to be able to fully utilize the available capacity. Undercapacity and overcapacity are equally undesirable. Ask this question:

Does the company presently have appropriate capacity for this item?

The answer is scored on this scale:

1 = No capacity whatever.

5 = Capacity is available, but timing is problematical.

10 = Off-peak or off-season capacity is both available and highly desirable for this item.

Factor Weights by Industry Groups — Capacity

Industry Group	Factor Weight	Industry Group	Factor Weight
Agriculture	1	Wholesale and Retail Trade	1
Mining	1	Finance, Insurance, Real Estate	1
Contract Construction	1	Services	1
Manufacturing	1	Government	1
Transportation	1		

Location. A common rule of thumb in real estate is that there are three major factors that determine the value and appreciation potential of a property for investment purposes: location, location, and location. The location of a company's facilities for doing business is equally important in a competitive sense, since it determines, or at least influences, so many of the other important factors. It is extremely difficult to maintain a competitive position in almost any industry unless the facility is easily accessible to critical resources or markets. The question to be asked is:

How competitively located is the company?

Answers are rated:

1 = Seriously disadvantaged, both for critical resources and markets.

5 = Equal to average competition.

10 = On balance, company has great competitive locational advantages with respect to both resources and markets.

Factor Weights by Industry Groups — Location			
Industry Group	Factor Weight	Industry Group	Factor Weight
Agriculture	2	Wholesale and Retail Trade	2
Mining	2	Finance, Insurance, Real Estate	1
Contract Construction	1	Services	2
Manufacturing	1	Government	2
Transportation	2		

Management. Bad management is by far the major cause of all business failures. Bad management may be difficult to recognize, and it is always difficult to admit. There is always some other "reason" for business failure that can be used to explain a company's poor showing, whether in the marketplace or in the shop, plant, or office. A company's production management holds the key to keeping production costs down, product quality up, and both costs and quality at a competitive level. The key question is:

Is the company's production management well suited for handling this item?

Answers score on this scale:

1 = No similar experience.

5 = Good experience controlling production of this general nature.

10 = Long and successful experience in production of items very similar to the proposed venture.

Factor Weights by Industry Groups—Management

Industry Group	Factor Weight	Industry Group	Factor Weight
Agriculture	1	Wholesale and Retail Trade	2
Mining	1	Finance, Insurance, Real Estate	1
Contract Construction	2	Services	1
Manufacturing	1	Government	1
Transportation	1		

Summary of Production Factors. The seven factors representing the company's capabilities for production of the proposed item can be summarized in these seven key questions:

1. *Labor*—how does the company's present labor situation compare with competitors?
2. *Facilities*—how do the company's facilities compare with competition?
3. *Purchasing*—how does the company's purchasing situation stack up against competition?
4. *Dependency*—to what extent is the company's production capability vulnerable in terms of overdependency?
5. *Capacity*—does the company presently have appropriate capacity for this item?
6. *Location*—how competitively located is the company?
7. *Management*—is the company's production management well suited for handling this item?

SUMMARY OF COMPANY FACTORS

The company's competitive strength is measured in the SAVE analysis by 20 factors falling in three factor groups. The factors are covered in the following questions, all relating to how well the company can handle the proposed venture:

1. *Marketing*. How much does the company have of what it takes to market the item effectively, as measured by its experience, support services, technical service, market coverage, entrenchment, dependency, volume, penetration, and management capabilities?
2. *Technology*. To what extent does the company have the technical know-how required for success in this venture, especially

with regard to design, engineering, materials, and techniques?

3. *Production.* Can the company produce the item competitively, based on its competitive position in terms of labor, facilities, purchasing, dependency, capacity, location, and management?

The SAVE rating sheet for company factors is presented in Fig. 4-2.

Factor	Factor Rating	Factor Weight	Factor Score	Factor Group	Factor Group Score
Experience	___	___	___		
Support Services	___	___	___		
Technical Service	___	___	___		
Market Coverage	___	___	___		
Entrenchment	___	___	___	Marketing	___
Dependency	___	___	___		
Volume	___	___	___		
Penetration	___	___	___		
Management	___	___	___		
Design	___	___	___		
Engineering	___	___	___		
Materials	___	___	___	Technology	___
Techniques	___	___	___		
Labor	___	___	___		
Facilities	___	___	___		
Purchasing	___	___	___		
Dependency	___	___	___	Production	___
Capacity	___	___	___		
Location	___	___	___		
Management	___	___	___		

Total Company Score
Total Score Possible
Company Efficiency Percentage

Fig. 4-2. SAVE rating sheet for company factors.

The factor scores and company efficiency percentages are determined in exactly the same manner as explained previously for the item factors, except that the maximum possible company scores by industry groups are different, as follows:

Maximum Possible Score				
Industry Group	Marketing	Technology	Production	Total
Agriculture	90	70	90	250
Mining	90	90	100	280
Contract Construction	110	60	80	250
Manufacturing	90	40	70	200
Transportation	100	50	80	230
Wholesale and Retail Trade	110	40	100	250
Finance, Insurance, Real Estate	110	40	70	220
Services	130	50	90	270
Government	130	50	80	260

As discussed before, low efficiency percentages should be viewed skeptically and the weak areas strengthened before moving ahead with the new venture. To ignore obvious weaknesses is to invite a financial disaster.

THE VENTURER WITHOUT A COMPANY

As shown in the preceding sections of this chapter, the strength of the venturing company is one of the most important aspects that determines success in a new business venture. Regardless of how good an idea is, and of how favorable the environment is for that idea, a large, well-established company has an obvious advantage over an individual in converting that idea into a successful business.

Even so, many new ventures do not involve an established company. Instead, much of their success depends on an individual entrepreneur, or at most, a few individual entrepreneurs. The company itself, lacking any established marketing, production, or technical experience, must therefore rely on the capabilities, characteristics, and expertise that these few individuals bring to the venture at hand.

Just as there are 20 major factors that measure the company's capabilities in marketing, technology, and production, there are 20 major characteristics of the venturer or entrepreneur that will ultimately determine the success or failure of a new venture. These characteristics can all be grouped into three broad categories:

1. Personal traits,
2. Know-how, and
3. Additional strengths.

The overall structure of the venturer's important characteristics, as defined in these 20 specific factors, is illustrated in Fig. 4-3.

These characteristics are all related to whether or not the involved individual or individuals have the specific capabilities required to succeed in this particular enterprise.

In the SAVE analysis, the venturer factors may be substituted for the company factors when they are considered to be more appropriate for the situation being analyzed, particularly for a new venture being considered or started up by an individual. The four major aspects then become: (1) the item, (2) the venturer, (3) the environment, and (4) the venture. Everything else is handled in exactly the same way as if a major established company were involved in the new venture.

PERSONAL TRAITS

Certain personal traits are required for success in any business, and especially in a new business venture. Seven specific traits have been identified as being particularly important in a new business venture:

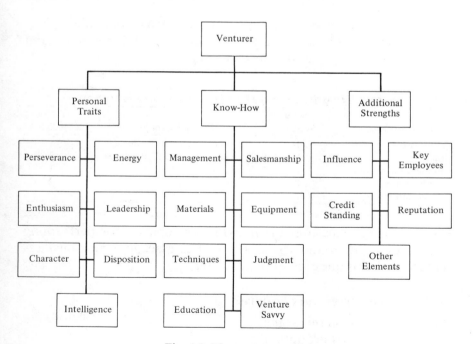

Fig. 4-3. The venturer model.

1. Perseverance,
2. Energy,
3. Enthusiasm,
4. Leadership,
5. Character,
6. Disposition, and
7. Intelligence.

Each of these traits will be briefly discussed in the following sections.

Perseverance. Perseverance measures the individual's ability to persist in whatever enterprise he undertakes, despite opposition or counterinfluences. The question is:

Does he see things through?

The answer is scored as follows:

1 = Record shows a tendency to give up or lose interest quite easily.

5 = Record shows good staying power when it counts.

10 = Record shows exceptionally strong motivation pattern, and persistence is a well-developed habit.

Factor Weights by Industry Groups — Perseverance			
Industry Group	Factor Weight	Industry Group	Factor Weight
Agriculture	1	Wholesale and Retail Trade	1
Mining	1	Finance, Insurance, Real Estate	2
Contract Construction	1	Services	1
Manufacturing	1	Government	2
Transportation	1		

Energy. Energy measures the individual's capacity for performing work with strength and vigor, an obvious asset in a new business venture. Ask this question of the venturer:

How much energy does he have?

Rate the answers on this scale:

1 = Seems to lack initiative.

5 = His energy probably matches his competition.

10 = Obviously has outstanding energy and drive.

Factor Weights by Industry Groups — Energy

Industry Group	Factor Weight	Industry Group	Factor Weight
Agriculture	1	Wholesale and Retail Trade	1
Mining	1	Finance, Insurance, Real Estate	1
Contract Construction	1	Services	1
Manufacturing	1	Government	1
Transportation	1		

Enthusiasm. Enthusiasm for a new venture is indicated by a keen and ardent interest in the project. Enthusiasm may be infectious, creating a comparable excitement and optimism among others involved in the enterprise. Too much enthusiasm, on the other hand, may result in a subordination of judgment. The question is:

Does he have the enthusiasm needed?

The ratings are based on this scale:

1 = Shows no apparent enthusiasm for the venture.

5 = Enthusiasm is normal, or about what might be expected.

10 = Very strong and infectious enthusiasm about the venture.

Factor Weights by Industry Groups — Enthusiasm

Industry Group	Factor Weight	Industry Group	Factor Weight
Agriculture	1	Wholesale and Retail Trade	1
Mining	1	Finance, Insurance, Real Estate	1
Contract Construction	1	Services	1
Manufacturing	1	Government	1
Transportation	1		

Leadership. Leadership is the quality of being able to guide or direct the actions, thoughts, and opinions of others—an important consideration in any business that involves a number of people. Here, the question is:

Does he have the required leadership qualities?

The answers rate as follows:

1 = His lack of self-confidence is an obvious and important disadvantage.

5 = His leadership ability is apparently adequate for this type of venture.

10 = His extraordinary leadership capability would be a very valuable asset.

Factor Weights by Industry Groups — Leadership

Industry Group	Factor Weight	Industry Group	Factor Weight
Agriculture	1	Wholesale and Retail Trade	1
Mining	1	Finance, Insurance, Real Estate	1
Contract Construction	1	Services	1
Manufacturing	1	Government	1
Transportation	1		

Character. Character is sometimes defined as "what you do when no one is looking." It implies a moral evaluation, encompassing a number of distinctive qualities and traits such as behavior, habits, self-discipline, reputation, moral firmness, honesty, and other characteristics. Somehow, this question must be answered:

Is he of sound character?

The rating scale is:

1 = Recent record suggests severe problems here.

5 = Record indicates no significant moral problems.

10 = His outstanding record would be an enormous advantage in this venture.

Factor Weights by Industry Groups — Character

Industry Group	Factor Weight	Industry Group	Factor Weight
Agriculture	1	Wholesale and Retail Trade	1
Mining	1	Finance, Insurance, Real Estate	1
Contract Construction	1	Services	1
Manufacturing	1	Government	1
Transportation	1		

Disposition. Disposition has to do with the individual's temperament or frame of mind which enables him to accept or react appropriately, but not excessively, to whatever situations confront him in the new venture. A very nervous person, for example, would perhaps be overwhelmed by a business normally encountering one crisis after another, and a careless person could not handle a business requiring great precision and order. Ask this question:

Does his disposition favor the venture?

Rate the answers on this scale:

1 = His disposition is an obvious and important disadvantage.
5 = His disposition seems appropriate for the venture.
10 = His disposition is exceptionally appropriate for this type of enterprise.

Factor Weights by Industry Groups—Disposition

Industry Group	Factor Weight	Industry Group	Factor Weight
Agriculture	1	Wholesale and Retail Trade	1
Mining	1	Finance, Insurance, Real Estate	1
Contract Construction	1	Services	1
Manufacturing	1	Government	1
Transportation	1		

Intelligence. In psychology, intelligence is defined as the ability of an individual to adapt to changes in his environment. In business, this translates into his ability to understand and interpret business information as a guide to action toward a desired goal, and to be able to meet and adjust to whatever unusual situations might arise. This question should be asked of the venturer:

Does he have the intelligence needed for success in this venture?

The answers are scored on this scale:

1 = His lack of intelligence would be a severe handicap.
5 = Intelligence is probably above average and equal to his competition.
10 = Outstanding intelligence where that would be an important advantage over competition.

		Factor Weights by Industry Groups—Intelligence		
Industry Group	Factor Weight		Industry Group	Factor Weight
Agriculture	1		Wholesale and Retail Trade	1
Mining	1		Finance, Insurance, Real Estate	1
Contract Construction	1		Services	1
Manufacturing	1		Government	1
Transportation	1			

Summary of Venturer Personal Trait Factors. The factors relating to the personal traits and characteristics of the individual venturer or venturers are among the most difficult to rate objectively. Nevertheless, they must be questioned and evaluated in the following manner:

1. *Perseverance*—does he see things through?
2. *Energy*—how much energy does he have?
3. *Enthusiasm*—does he have the enthusiasm needed?
4. *Leadership*—does he have the required leadership qualities?
5. *Character*—is he of sound character?
6. *Disposition*—does his disposition favor the venture?
7. *Intelligence*—does he have the intelligence needed for success in this venture?

KNOW-HOW

The individual entering a new business venture must have a certain level of knowledge, experience, and judgment relevant to the business. Eight factors measure the extent to which the venturer has the know-how he needs in order to be successful in the enterprise.

1. Management,
2. Salesmanship,
3. Materials,
4. Equipment,
5. Techniques,
6. Judgment,
7. Education, and
8. Venture Savvy.

Several of these factors are the same as those included among the company factors. Whether the venturer is an individual or an established company, there are some obvious similarities in a number of the factors contributing to a successful business venture.

Management. Bad management causes far more business failures than bad luck. The ability to judiciously and skillfully control and direct all of the many business functions required in even the smallest of businesses is a critical necessity. This ability can only be proven in practice. The question concerning the venturer is:

Is he a good manager?

The answers are rated:

1 = Has shown a continuous pattern of serious problems in managing his money, personal affairs, time, or other matters.

5 = Has shown substantial ability to control his affairs.

10 = Has shown exceptional ability to organize and manage a business enterprise of the proposed type.

Factor Weights by Industry Groups—Management

Industry Group	Factor Weight	Industry Group	Factor Weight
Agriculture	1	Wholesale and Retail Trade	2
Mining	1	Finance, Insurance, Real Estate	1
Contract Construction	2	Services	2
Manufacturing	1	Government	1
Transportation	1		

Salesmanship. Being able to sell his product, his service, or himself is a real gift and a valuable asset in any business. To succeed in selling requires a dedicated ambition to be willing to make sacrifices to help people—a dedication that few people have. It also requires a knowledge of selling techniques appropriate to the item being sold. Ask of the venturer:

Does he have the selling abilities required to be successful in this type of venture?

Rate the answers:

1 = His lack of selling ability and experience would be a very important disadvantage compared with competition.

5 = His selling experience and ability are probably adequate to meet competition on fairly even terms.

10 = He is an exceptionally successful salesman in this field, and this will be a great advantage over his competition.

Factor Weights by Industry Groups—Salesmanship

Industry Group	Factor Weight	Industry Group	Factor Weight
Agriculture	1	Wholesale and Retail Trade	2
Mining	1	Finance, Insurance, Real Estate	2
Contract Construction	1	Services	1
Manufacturing	1	Government	1
Transportation	1		

Materials. A knowledge of the materials involved in the proposed business venture is as important for an individual venturer as it is for an established company. Here, the question is simply:

Is he experienced with the materials involved in this venture?

The answers rate as follows:

1 = He has no related experience whatever.

5 = He has adequate related experience and a sound understanding of the materials involved.

10 = His knowledge of the materials constitutes an extremely important advantage over competition.

Factor Weights by Industry Groups—Materials

Industry Group	Factor Weight	Industry Group	Factor Weight
Agriculture	2	Wholesale and Retail Trade	1
Mining	3	Finance, Insurance, Real Estate	1
Contract Construction	1	Services	1
Manufacturing	1	Government	1
Transportation	1		

Equipment. As with materials, a thorough familiarity with the equipment or tools of his trade is important, whether the tools consist of complex machinery, hand tools, or computers. Ask this question of the venturer:

How well does he understand the equipment which is used in this venture?

Score the answers as follows:

1 = He has no knowledge of such equipment.

5 = He has good basic experience with such equipment and can probably match his competition.

10 = His expert knowledge of equipment used in this business gives him a great competitive advantage.

Factor Weights by Industry Groups — Equipment			
Industry Group	Factor Weight	Industry Group	Factor Weight
Agriculture	2	Wholesale and Retail Trade	1
Mining	2	Finance, Insurance, Real Estate	1
Contract Construction	2	Services	2
Manufacturing	1	Government	1
Transportation	2		

Techniques. Techniques refer to the specific methods and details of the procedures which are essential in the successful conduct of any business enterprise. A sound knowledge of the appropriate techniques for the business being considered is obviously important. Ask:

Is he experienced in the techniques and methods used in this kind of enterprise?

The answers are scored as follows:

1 = He has no knowledge of the techniques involved.

5 = He probably understands the basic techniques as well as his average competition.

10 = He has expert knowledge of the techniques in all phases of the proposed operation, and this gives him an important advantage over his competition.

Factor Weights by Industry Groups — Techniques			
Industry Group	Factor Weight	Industry Group	Factor Weight
Agriculture	3	Wholesale and Retail Trade	1
Mining	3	Finance, Insurance, Real Estate	1
Contract Construction	3	Services	2
Manufacturing	1	Government	2
Transportation	2		

Judgment. Judgment, in a business sense, reflects the individual's ability to arrive at a wise and correct business decision. Such decisions normally involve comparison and discrimination, by which a knowledge of values and relationships can be mentally formulated. Good business judgment is hard to come by, and is always in great demand. Ask:

Does he have sound business judgment?

The answers are scored:

   1 = He has a serious lack of good business judgment.

   5 = His judgment seems adequate and would probably be equal to competition; he learns the facts needed for decisions.

  10 = He has remarkably well-balanced judgment which would probably be an important advantage over competition.

Factor Weights by Industry Groups — Judgment			
Industry Group	Factor Weight	Industry Group	Factor Weight
Agriculture	1	Wholesale and Retail Trade	2
Mining	2	Finance, Insurance, Real Estate	1
Contract Construction	1	Services	1
Manufacturing	1	Government	1
Transportation	1		

Education. Education implies a mental discipline obtained through study or instruction. Usually, business education need not be of a formal nature; formal college-level business courses, in fact, are not noted for being particularly useful to the entrepreneurial mind, but are oriented more toward the corporate employee-manager. In technical fields, though, structured study may be important, and important business skills such as accounting, marketing, and law can be best acquired in this manner. The important point is simply that the venturer's education be appropriate for the proposed venture. Ask:

Is his education adequate for this venture?

The answers rate:

   1 = His lack of education would be a very serious disadvantage.

5 = His education either in school or by self-taught means is adequate to meet his competition on equal terms.

10 = He is extremely well educated for this kind of venture, and this would be a great advantage over his competition.

Factor Weights by Industry Groups — Education

Industry Group	Factor Weight	Industry Group	Factor Weight
Agriculture	1	Wholesale and Retail Trade	1
Mining	2	Finance, Insurance, Real Estate	1
Contract Construction	1	Services	2
Manufacturing	1	Government	1
Transportation	1		

Venture Savvy. The term *savvy* implies a practical knowledge and understanding of the venture being undertaken, something beyond the knowledge gained through formal education. It is, essentially, a common-sense ability to handle whatever problems might arise in the business. This is the question:

How well does he understand the problems and pitfalls of undertaking such a business venture?

The answers to this question cover the range:

1 = Has no business experience of any kind, and seems to have a serious lack of understanding about the problems involved.

5 = Has investigated this kind of venture thoroughly and is familiar with its major problems.

10 = Has actively participated in this kind of venture before, knows the problems and how to solve them, and seems to avoid pitfalls instinctively.

Factor Weights by Industry Groups — Venture Savvy

Industry Group	Factor Weight	Industry Group	Factor Weight
Agriculture	1	Wholesale and Retail Trade	1
Mining	2	Finance, Insurance, Real Estate	1
Contract Construction	2	Services	2
Manufacturing	1	Government	2
Transportation	1		

Summary of Venturer Know-How Factors. The eight factors falling in this category are designed to measure the extent to which the venturer has the know-how he needs to be successful in the proposed business enterprise. The factors that describe his know-how are:

1. *Management*—is he a good manager?
2. *Salesmanship*—does he have the selling abilities required to be successful in this type of business?
3. *Materials*—is he experienced with the materials involved in this venture?
4. *Equipment*—how well does he understand the equipment which is used in this venture?
5. *Techniques*—is he experienced in the techniques and methods used in this kind of enterprise?
6. *Judgment*—does he have sound business judgment?
7. *Education*—is his education adequate for this venture?
8. *Venture Savvy*—how well does he understand the problems and pitfalls of undertaking this business venture?

ADDITIONAL STRENGTHS

In addition to his personal characteristics and his acquired know-how, the venturer may have other special advantages or disadvantages which will bear upon the success of the new business. Five specific factors are included in this category:

1. Influence,
2. Key employees,
3. Credit standing,
4. Reputation, and
5. Other.

Influence. There can be no doubt that who you know, as well as what you know, can play an important role in the success of any business venture. Having an inside track through personal connections with major customers or markets, or having political influence that will ease some of the problems associated with a new business, are especially important during the start-up phase. Here is the appropriate question:

Does he have any special connections or friends who will enhance the prospects of success for this venture?

Answers rate as follows:

1 = Good connections are highly desirable, but not available.

5 = Connections are either adequate or unnecessary.

10 = Connections are extremely powerful and can be counted upon to exert substantial influence on behalf of this venture.

Factor Weights by Industry Groups — Influence

Industry Group	Factor Weight	Industry Group	Factor Weight
Agriculture	1	Wholesale and Retail Trade	1
Mining	1	Finance, Insurance, Real Estate	1
Contract Construction	1	Services	1
Manufacturing	1	Government	3
Transportation	1		

Key Employees. Every business venture, no matter how small, requires a certain level of competence in a number of different disciplines. If the entrepreneur lacks competence in any of these areas, he must either acquire the necessary competence himself, or hire competent people to handle the tasks. Having just a few highly competent individuals can make a big difference in the business. Ask:

Does he have competent people available for key participation in the venture?

The answers rate as follows:

1 = Good associates are needed, but none are available.

5 = The most critical responsibilities are adequately manned.

10 = Exceptionally competent people are available for all key responsibilities.

Factor Weights by Industry Groups — Key Employees

Industry Group	Factor Weight	Industry Group	Factor Weight
Agriculture	1	Wholesale and Retail Trade	1
Mining	1	Finance, Insurance, Real Estate	1
Contract Construction	1	Services	2
Manufacturing	1	Government	1
Transportation	1		

Credit Standing. Without an established credit history, suppliers are understandably reluctant to extend open credit lines to new businesses. This means that payment will be required either with order or on delivery, thus complicating the purchasing procedure and greatly increasing the working capital requirements of the business. A bad credit rating is a serious competitive disadvantage. Check the following:

To what extent is the venturer's business credit standing favorable and well established?

The answers can be very revealing:

1 = Very unfavorable record.

5 = No record at all; not even a personal credit history has been established.

6 = Responsible personal credit history has been established.

10 = He has been bonded and has established an outstanding business credit rating; rated highly by Dun & Bradstreet, with good credit and bank references.

	Factor Weights by Industry Groups—Credit Standing		
Industry Group	Factor Weight	Industry Group	Factor Weight
Agriculture	1	Wholesale and Retail Trade	2
Mining	1	Finance, Insurance, Real Estate	1
Contract Construction	1	Services	1
Manufacturing	1	Government	1
Transportation	1		

Reputation. A man's reputation is like his shadow: sometimes it follows him, sometimes it precedes him, sometimes it is taller than he is, and sometimes it is shorter. His reputation actually represents others' opinions regarding his character, whether or not these opinions are based on fact. The effect of the individual's personal reputation on the success of the new venture should be seriously questioned:

Will the venturer's personal reputation significantly affect the venture's success?

Answers rate as follows:

1 = Seriously unfavorable factor.

5 = No particular effect at all.
10 = Extremely advantageous effect.

Factor Weights by Industry Groups—Reputation

Industry Group	Factor Weight	Industry Group	Factor Weight
Agriculture	1	Wholesale and Retail Trade	2
Mining	1	Finance, Insurance, Real Estate	1
Contract Construction	1	Services	2
Manufacturing	1	Government	1
Transportation	1		

Other. A real professional—whether in business, sports, or any other field—will not let his problems in any one area affect his performance in other areas. Family problems, for example, will not impair his effectiveness in business, and financial problems will not cause him to mistreat his family. Nevertheless, not all people are able to isolate their problems in this way, and this question should be examined:

How may other personal factors, such as health, physical strength, and family situation, be expected to affect success in the proposed venture?

The expected effects are rated:
1 = Important disadvantages here.
5 = On balance, no net effect either way.
10 = Important advantages here.

Factor Weights by Industry Groups—Other

Industry Group	Factor Weight	Industry Group	Factor Weight
Agriculture	2	Wholesale and Retail Trade	1
Mining	1	Finance, Insurance, Real Estate	1
Contract Construction	1	Services	1
Manufacturing	1	Government	2
Transportation	2		

Summary of Venturer Additional Strengths Factors. Factors included in this category incorporate a number of considerations beyond the individual venturer's personal traits and technical know-how. The five additional factors all relate to whether the venturer has any other special advantages or disadvantages which could be expected to bear upon the success of the particular business being considered. They are:

1. *Influence*—does he have any special connections or friends who will enhance the prospects of success for this venture?
2. *Key Employees*—does he have competent people available for key participation in the venture?
3. *Credit Standing*—to what extent is the venturer's business credit standing favorable and well established?
4. *Reputation*—will the venturer's personal reputation significantly affect the venture's success?
5. *Other*—how may other personal factors, such as health, physical strength, and family situation, be expected to affect success in the proposed venture?

SUMMARY OF VENTURER FACTORS

The "venturer' is used as the second of the four major aspects affecting the success of a new business venture when the venture is being undertaken by an individual rather than by an already-established company. In such cases, the "company" aspect is simply disregarded and replaced in the SAVE analysis by the "venturer" aspect.

The venturer factors are designed to reveal whether the venturer has the capabilities required for the particular enterprise being considered. The 20 individual factors in this category are divided into three factor groups, as follows:

1. *Personal Traits.* Does the venturer possess the personal traits required for success, including perseverance, energy, enthusiasm, leadership, character, disposition, and intelligence?
2. *Know-How.* To what extent does the venturer have the know-how he needs to be successful in this enterprise, with respect to management, salesmanship, materials, equipment, techniques, judgment, education, and venture savvy?
3. *Additional Strengths.* Does the venturer have other special advantages or disadvantages which might bear upon the success of this business, such as influence, key employees, credit standing, reputation, or other considerations?

Factor	Factor Rating	Factor Weight	Factor Score	Factor Group	Factor Group Score
Perseverance	_____	_____	_____		
Energy	_____	_____	_____		
Enthusiasm	_____	_____	_____	Personal	
Leadership	_____	_____	_____	Traits	_____
Character	_____	_____	_____		
Disposition	_____	_____	_____		
Intelligence	_____	_____	_____		
Management	_____	_____	_____		
Salesmanship	_____	_____	_____		
Materials	_____	_____	_____		
Equipment	_____	_____	_____		
Techniques	_____	_____	_____	Know-How	_____
Judgment	_____	_____	_____		
Education	_____	_____	_____		
Venture Savvy	_____	_____	_____		
Influence	_____	_____	_____		
Key Employees	_____	_____	_____		
Credit Standing	_____	_____	_____	Additional	_____
Reputation	_____	_____	_____	Strengths	
Other	_____	_____	_____		
Total Venturer Score					
Total Score Possible					_____
Venturer Efficiency Percentage					_____

Fig. 4-4. SAVE rating sheet for venturer factors.

A SAVE rating sheet for the venturer factors is shown in Fig. 4-4.

The approach to determining factor scores and efficiency percentages has already been covered. For the venturer category, the maximum possible scores by major factor groups are as shown on p. 84 for the different industries.

Whether the venture is to be pursued by a company or an individual, a great deal of strength and competence in many diverse areas must be expected of the venturer in order to achieve any degree of success. Shortcomings identified in the individual venturer may, however, be considerably more difficult to overcome or strengthen than when an established company is involved. Severe uncorrectable deficiencies may, in the case of an individual, be sufficient cause to dictate a "no-go" decision.

Maximum Possible Score

Industry Group	Personal Traits	Know-How	Additional Strengths	Total
Agriculture	70	120	60	250
Mining	70	160	50	280
Contract Construction	70	130	50	250
Manufacturing	70	80	50	200
Transportation	70	100	60	230
Wholesale and Retail Trade	70	110	70	250
Finance, Insurance, Real Estate	80	90	50	220
Services	70	130	70	270
Government	80	100	80	260

5
The Environment

Environmental factors together account for between one-fourth and one-third of the success of a new business venture, and constitute the most important group of factors in most industries. Unfortunately, the environmental factors are those over which the venturing company has little or no direct control.

By definition, environmental factors include the aggregate of all the external conditions and influences that affect the survival and growth of the venture.

Although environmental factors cannot generally be controlled, most of them are either known or can be anticipated. Consequently, they can be incorporated as independent variables in the company's overall venture strategy, enabling the company to either take advantage of them or to minimize any harmful impacts.

The environmental factors affecting a new venture are broken into four broad categories:

1. Market,
2. Competition,
3. Suppliers, and
4. Government.

These four categories of factors determine the supply and demand situation with respect to the contemplated item, establish the share of market that can be attained, and define the rules under which the venture must operate. Without an environment favorable to the item, there is very little chance of venture success regardless of the item's characteristics and the company's capabilities.

Figure 5-1 shows the structure of the environment category.

MARKET

A strong market is required for a successful venture in any field. Even the best product, supported by the strongest company with virtually unlimited resources and capabilities, will die in the marketplace if there is insufficient consumer demand. Many new businesses have failed because the enthusiasm of the venturer was found to be unmatched by any corresponding level of enthusiasm in the marketplace.

The size of a market is only one of a number of considerations. Highly successful ventures can be launched in markets of limited size, providing the limitations are recognized, understood, and accepted in advance.

The important market-related factors to be considered in this category include these six topics:

1. Potential volume,
2. Proportion,
3. Fertility,
4. Growth,
5. Stability, and
6. Outlook.

All six factors are aimed at determining whether there is a good, or at least adequate, market for the proposed item.

Potential Volume. The total national sales volume of the proposed item is an important figure in an informational sense, even if not critical from the standpoint of operational success. The total volume, combined with competitive considerations, determines the share of market that can be realistically attained, and thereby defines the volume potential for the new venture. Abundant data are usually available from published sources to at least gain some appreciation of the overall market picture for almost anything, whether product or service. A simple but useful approach to estimating the

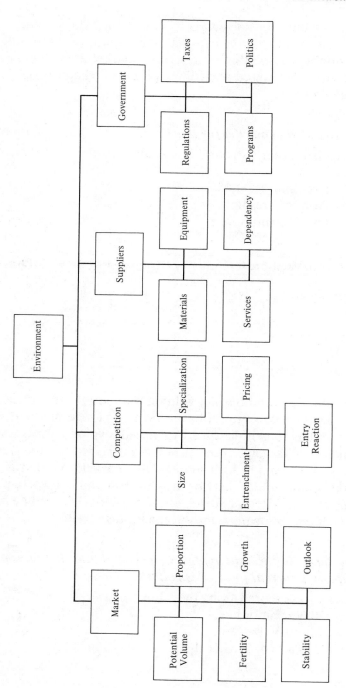

Fig. 5-1. The environment model.

potential volume for an item is to obtain the total national volume for the item, divide by the national population, then multiply by the population located within a prescribed market area. The important question to be answered regarding volume in whatever field is being investigated is:

Is there a strong market for this item?

While realizing that "strong" is a subjective term, rate the answers as follows:

1 = Less than $200,000.
5 = About $2 million.
10 = Over $20 million.

Factor Weights by Industry Groups—Potential Volume

Industry Group	Factor Weight	Industry Group	Factor Weight
Agriculture	1	Wholesale and Retail Trade	1
Mining	1	Finance, Insurance, Real Estate	1
Contract Construction	1	Services	1
Manufacturing	1	Government	2
Transportation	1		

Proportion. Potential market volume is an important consideration in the new business venture, but it must be viewed in a realistic perspective. What constitutes an adequate sales volume for a new enterprise depends largely upon the characteristics of the venturing company. What might be a tremendous market volume for a small company to add could easily be insignificant and not worth pursuing by a large firm. After a realistic estimate of market volume has been developed, the following question can be answered:

How large is the anticipated market volume in relation to the company's current total sales volume?

The answers are scored along these lines:

1 = 20 percent or less.
5 = About 50 percent.
10 = Equal to or greater than present volume.

Factor Weights by Industry Groups — Proportion			
Industry Group	Factor Weight	Industry Group	Factor Weight
Agriculture ·	1	Wholesale and Retail Trade	1
Mining	1	Finance, Insurance, Real Estate	1
Contract Construction	1	Services	1
Manufacturing	1	Government	0
Transportation	1		

Fertility. Fertility, as its name implies, refers to how well the pro-posed new venture can take root and grow in its environment, given the best of care. Some new items that can be nurtured into success by aggressive promotional and marketing programs might otherwise die in the marketplace if left to make it on their own. The question is:

What share of the total market volume could the proposed item displace or capture at a saturation level of marketing effort in all areas, unlimited by cost?

Answers rate as follows:

  1 = 10 percent or less.
  5 = About 50 percent.
 10 = 90 percent or more.

Factor Weights by Industry Groups — Fertility			
Industry Group	Factor Weight	Industry Group	Factor Weight
Agriculture	1	Wholesale and Retail Trade	1
Mining	1	Finance, Insurance, Real Estate	1
Contract Construction	1	Services	1
Manufacturing	1	Government	0
Transportation	1		

Growth. An expanding market is essential for new venture success. Otherwise, any volume attained must be taken away from estab-lished firms—at best an uncertain and difficult task. Growth in dol-lar volume is meaningful only when compared with the nation's economy as a whole; during periods of high inflation, percentage growth rates can be deceiving and even items experiencing actual de-clines in terms of physical units can appear to be growing in dollar sales. The important question is:

How much is the market expanding each year?

Answers are scored on this scale:

  1 = Real market volume is not growing at all.

  5 = Real growth rate matches that of the national economy.

10 = Real growth rate is at least three to four times that of the nation's economy as a whole.

		Factor Weights by Industry Groups — Growth		
Industry Group	Factor Weight	Industry Group	Factor Weight
Agriculture	1	Wholesale and Retail Trade	1
Mining	1	Finance, Insurance, Real Estate	1
Contract Construction	1	Services	1
Manufacturing	1	Government	2
Transportation	1		

Stability. Stability or predictability of the market for a new product or service is a very desirable market attribute. Most markets experience certain seasonal or cyclical fluctuations, but these are generally normal variations that can be anticipated and incorporated in the business plan. Seasonally oriented markets are, in fact, advantageous to the firm that has other items with different seasonal or cyclical characteristics. Wildly fluctuating market demands, though, are not conducive to new item success, and should be viewed with caution and the following question:

How constant is the demand for this item?

Answers to this question are rated as follows:

  1 = Fluctuations are sharp and unpredictable, both seasonally and cyclically.

  5 = Fluctuations are moderate and normal.

10 = Fluctuations are moderate and tend to be contraseasonal and contracyclical compared with the company's other markets.

		Factor Weights by Industry Groups — Stability		
Industry Group	Factor Weight	Industry Group	Factor Weight
Agriculture	2	Wholesale and Retail Trade	2
Mining	2	Finance, Insurance, Real Estate	1
Contract Construction	1	Services	1
Manufacturing	1	Government	0
Transportation	1		

Outlook. Many items have interesting life cycles, and knowing where an item stands in its own life cycle is an important consideration. The conventional life cycle curve shows slow early growth as the new item trys to get established, followed by a period of rapid growth as it catches on, slowing as it approaches saturation, and finally decreasing in its last declining stages. The main consideration here is to be certain that the proposed item is located at a point on its life cycle curve that allows some upside potential. Ask:

How great and enduring is the future demand for such items?

Score the answers on this scale:

  1 = Substantial vulnerability to known threats or changes in the immediate future; future potential is limited.

  5 = Outlook seems normal; no particular deterioration foreseen.

10 = Demand is on the verge of a strong acceleration for reliable reasons; future potential is immense.

Factor Weights by Industry Groups — Outlook

Industry Group	Factor Weight	Industry Group	Factor Weight
Agriculture	1	Wholesale and Retail Trade	1
Mining	1	Finance, Insurance, Real Estate	1
Contract Construction	1	Services	1
Manufacturing	1	Government	2
Transportation	1		

Summary of Market Factors. The six market factors considered in this category are intended to clarify the market characteristics of the proposed item. These factors cover the following points:

1. *Potential Volume*—is there a strong market for this item?
2. *Proportion*—how large is the anticipated market volume in relation to the company's current total sales volume?
3. *Fertility*—what share of the total market volume could the proposed item displace or capture at a saturation level of marketing effort in all areas, unlimited by cost?
4. *Growth*—how much is the market expanding each year?
5. *Stability*—how constant is the demand for this item?
6. *Outlook*—how great and enduring is the future demand for such items?

COMPETITION

Competition is one of the facts of business life. It is not necessarily bad, since competition indicates that a market really exists and that there are customers out there somewhere. It is important, though, to know the competition—who they are, where they are, and what they are doing.

The direct costs associated with providing a particular product or service generally determine the lower limit of prices. The upper limit on prices is established by competition.

In extremely competitive situations, such as are usually encountered in the contract construction industry and are often found in manufacturing, retail, and other fields, competitive factors may constitute an overwhelming consideration. In fact, the business may find itself in one of two extreme positions because of competitor's bidding or pricing practices:

1. Pricing the goods or services so low, in order to sell them at competitive price levels, that there will be virtually no profit regardless of the sales volume achieved, or

2. Pricing the goods or services so high, in order to realize a profit on them, that there will be virtually no volume because of consumer price resistance.

Competitive factors must be considered in any business situation, since they largely determine the price/volume relationships of any new item. The specific factors included in this category are:

1. Size,
2. Specialization,
3. Entrenchment,
4. Pricing, and
5. Entry reaction.

These five factors will answer the important questions regarding the type of competition currently dominating the market under consideration.

Size. The size of competitive firms offering items related to the proposed new venture is important only in relationship to the company's own size. In fields dominated by large firms, small firms can expect problems in competing effectively; conversely, in fields dominated by small firms, large firms might be wise to either stay out or to carefully check the reasons why their potential competitors are all small. The important consideration is that the company be an appropriate size for the new item, and the question is:

How large is the typical competitor, compared with your company?

Answers are rated on this scale:

1 = All competitors are either much larger or much smaller.
5 = About one-half of the total market is supplied by firms approximately the same size as yours.
10 = Companies your size supply the entire market.

Factor Weights by Industry Groups — Size			
Industry Group	Factor Weight	Industry Group	Factor Weight
Agriculture	2	Wholesale and Retail Trade	2
Mining	3	Finance, Insurance, Real Estate	1
Contract Construction	2	Services	2
Manufacturing	1	Government	1
Transportation	1		

Specialization. Increasing specialization is becoming more and more a reality of business. In view of this competitive environment, it can be a real advantage to a company, though, to be able to offer a variety of companion items, especially when a new item is introduced. The capability of providing customers and clients with associated products or services substantially expands the company's overall markets without adding corresponding costs, and greatly enhances the new item's chances for success. In evaluating the specialization factor, ask:

To what extent are other firms specializing in this item to the exclusion of companion items?

Rate the answers as follows:

1 = Most competitors have complete lines of associated items.
5 = About one-half of the total market is supplied by narrow specialists.

10 = The market is entirely supplied by firms who specialize in this item.

Factor Weights by Industry Groups — Specialization

Industry Group	Factor Weight	Industry Group	Factor Weight
Agriculture	1	Wholesale and Retail Trade	2
Mining	1	Finance, Insurance, Real Estate	1
Contract Construction	1	Services	1
Manufacturing	1	Government	1
Transportation	3		

Entrenchment. Firmly entrenched competitors are difficult to displace, regardless of any advantages the proposed new item might have. Even attempting to break into a field that is dominated by large firms with good reputations and solid trade support in their fields constitutes a hazardous and questionable business venture. In some areas, though, major customers for an item welcome, or even actively solicit, new sources for the item. Ask this question:

How deeply entrenched in the trade are the competitors?

Answers are scaled on this basis:

1 = Market is absolutely dominated by firms who are well known and highly regarded by trade accounts and/or customers.

5 = Important customers welcome new alternate sources.

10 = Important customers are intensively seeking new sources.

Factor Weights by Industry Groups — Entrenchment

Industry Group	Factor Weight	Industry Group	Factor Weight
Agriculture	1	Wholesale and Retail Trade	1
Mining	1	Finance, Insurance, Real Estate	1
Contract Construction	1	Services	1
Manufacturing	1	Government	2
Transportation	1		

Pricing. Industry price levels that generate high profit margins often attract new entries into the field, lured by the prospects of good profits in established markets. Prices generally reflect the intensity of competition within an industry. The contract construction field is probably the most price-sensitive industry; in competitive bidding, the highest price a company can get for a project is the lowest price at which its cheapest competitor is willing to take the job. Consumer goods and services are also extremely price-sensitive, while capital-intensive industries generally have a more structured and realistic pricing environment. Here, the question is:

How favorable is the traditional price behavior in this field?

Answers rate as follows:

  1 = Price pressure is constant and extremely severe.
  5 = Prices are competitive but generally well behaved.
 10 = Prices are usually maintained at very comfortable levels.

Factor Weights by Industry Groups — Pricing

Industry Group	Factor Weight	Industry Group	Factor Weight
Agriculture	1	Wholesale and Retail Trade	2
Mining	1	Finance, Insurance, Real Estate	1
Contract Construction	2	Services	2
Manufacturing	1	Government	1
Transportation	1		

Entry Reaction. Retaliatory measures taken by major competitors can destroy a new venture before it gets even a chance to make good, if the competitors are capable of and inclined toward such actions. If competitors control major supply sources, the company may well be vulnerable in this respect; if competitors lower prices, the company will be forced to follow suit; or, if competitors have strong influence with local government officials and agencies, real estate developers, utilities, or any other entities also having important inputs into the new venture, there is at least a potential for trouble. While new businesses are not generally welcomed by existing firms in the same field, most competitors will not overreact to a new entry unless they envision it as a real economic threat. Nevertheless, the possibility of competitive counteractions should be questioned:

What kind of competitive reaction will your entry into this field probably cause?

Answers rate on this scale:

1 = Entry will likely result in very harmful reactions of an important and permanent nature.

5 = Normal impact and response, but no reactions of great significance or permanence.

10 = No noticeable reaction whatever, or perhaps even favorable reactions such as business referrals and exchange of information.

Factor Weights by Industry Groups — Entry Reaction			
Industry Group	Factor Weight	Industry Group	Factor Weight
Agriculture	1	Wholesale and Retail Trade	1
Mining	1	Finance, Insurance, Real Estate	2
Contract Construction	1	Services	2
Manufacturing	1	Government	3
Transportation	2		

Summary of Competition Factors. The five factors included in this category are intended to define the overall competitive structure of the industry, and to identify some of the competitors' important characteristics. Answering these questions will provide the necessary background:

1. *Size*—how large is the typical competitor, compared with your company?
2. *Specialization*—to what extent are other firms specializing in this item to the exclusion of companion items?
3. *Entrenchment*—how deeply entrenched in the trade are the competitors?
4. *Pricing*—how favorable is the traditional price behavior in this market?
5. *Entry Reaction*—what kind of competitive reaction will your entry into this field probably cause?

SUPPLIERS

A business cannot exist without its suppliers. The company's vendors or suppliers can, in fact, be viewed as extensions of its production operations. The long-range objective of a company's relationships with its suppliers is to assure continuity and economy of supply.

Selecting the right source of supply and negotiating for the actual price are the two main functions of a company's purchasing program. The vendors are chosen on the basis of quality, cost, service, and other factors. Continuity of supply and competitiveness of prices on supplies, though, can be assured only by dealing with alternate or multiple supply sources. The ability to change supply sources quickly is the most powerful leverage that a company has on its supply costs.

Four major factors are considered in the *suppliers* category:

1. Materials,
2. Equipment,
3. Services, and
4. Dependency.

How well the industry is situated with respect to supplies and services will largely determine how effectively production can be planned and scheduled, critical factors in moving the item to its market.

Materials. Sources of materials, encompassing all of the company's supplies used in producing a salable item, are usually beyond the company's direct control. The materials in question may consist of raw materials used in a production process, or they may refer to the finished merchandise sold in a retail store or in a mail-order promotion. Regardless, if the venture requires materials in order to operate, the necessary materials must be available and competitively priced, and provision must be made to obtain them from alternative sources should the primary source be unable to deliver as required. The important question is:

Are the required supplies and components readily and consistently available in the desired qualities and quantities at reasonable prices?

Answers rate as follows:

1 = Shutdowns and changeovers due to supply shortages are common, and availability problems are increasing.

5 = Availability problems do arise, but can usually be resolved by anticipatory stockpiling.

10 = Materials are always available in complete ranges of quality and quantity with no problems whatsoever.

Factor Weights by Industry Groups — Materials

Industry Group	Factor Weight	Industry Group	Factor Weight
Agriculture	2	Wholesale and Retail Trade	2
Mining	1	Finance, Insurance, Real Estate	1
Contract Construction	2	Services	1
Manufacturing	1	Government	1
Transportation	2		

Equipment. The equipment required to conduct a business may include highly complex industrial machinery, highly specialized agricultural, mining, or construction equipment, extensive computer systems, and other types of sophisticated and expensive items. Or, it may consist of an adding machine, a typewriter, and a cash register. The important point is simply:

Is the required equipment always readily available?

Answers are rated on this scale:

1 = Shutdowns or temporary problems commonly arise because of equipment shortages or deficiencies.

5 = Equipment problems do arise, but equipment suppliers are attentive and respond quickly and effectively to customer needs.

10 = No problems whatsoever.

Factor Weights by Industry Groups — Equipment

Industry Group	Factor Weight	Industry Group	Factor Weight
Agriculture	2	Wholesale and Retail Trade	1
Mining	1	Finance, Insurance, Real Estate	1
Contract Construction	2	Services	1
Manufacturing	1	Government	1
Transportation	1		

Services. Few businesses can function effectively without a variety of support services. It is seldom economically feasible to provide many of these services in-house, so the company must depend on outside suppliers. The specific services that are important in a given industry may vary widely and may include information, transportation, printing, repair, finishing, or any number of other types of services. Some of the important considerations in selecting suppliers of services include factors such as these: ability to meet specifications, technical capabilities, performance, price, price stability, availability, location, ability to respond whenever needed, and many others. Regardless of the types of services needed, the basic question remains:

How well supported is the industry in terms of available services?
The answers are rated:

1 = At least one key type of service is extremely unreliable or chronically deficient.

5 = Service problems do arise, but the service industries are fair and responsive to industry problems.

10 = No problems whatsoever.

Factor Weights by Industry Groups—Services

Industry Group	Factor Weight	Industry Group	Factor Weight
Agriculture	2	Wholesale and Retail Trade	2
Mining	2	Finance, Insurance, Real Estate	1
Contract Construction	2	Services	2
Manufacturing	1	Government	1
Transportation	2		

Dependency. Just as human life is limited by whatever necessary resource is in most limited supply—air, water, food, space, etc.—a business's existence depends on whatever necessary resource is in most limited supply, such as energy, raw materials, personnel, customers, money, and so forth. If any one essential resource is lacking, the entire business will cease to exist, regardless of the availability of all other resources. When a company deals with only one source of supply for a critical item, competition is eliminated and any number of unfortunate circumstances could render the vendor inoperative, resulting in a shutdown of production. Ask:

To what extent are the industry's costs and operations dependent upon uncontrollable supply and/or service factors?

The answers rate as follows:

1 = Extremely sensitive and vulnerable to upstream or downstream work stoppages, and so forth.

5 = Industry's degree of dependency seems normal.

10 = The industry is completely independent of such factors.

Factor Weights by Industry Groups — Dependency

Industry Group	Factor Weight	Industry Group	Factor Weight
Agriculture	1	Wholesale and Retail Trade	1
Mining	1	Finance, Insurance, Real Estate	1
Contract Construction	1	Services	1
Manufacturing	1	Government	1
Transportation	1		

Summary of Suppliers Factors. The four factors included in the suppliers factor group may be critical to the success of a new venture, in that deficiencies in any area can halt the production process. These factors measure the industry's situation with respect to supplies and services:

1. *Materials*—are the required supplies and components readily and consistently available in the desired qualities and quantities at reasonable prices?
2. *Equipment*—is the required equipment always readily available?
3. *Services*—how well supported is the industry in terms of available services?
4. *Dependency*—to what extent are the industry's costs and operations dependent upon uncontrollable supply and/or service factors?

GOVERNMENT

The possible impact of government on any new venture cannot be overemphasized. Every government entity with any conceivable jurisdiction—federal, state, and local—will impose its regulations, controls, and taxes on the new business.

Government sets the rules by which the game of business must be played. The federal, state, and local governments all have the power to regulate business activities within their jurisdictions. A variety of legislation has been enacted at the federal level to protect competition, prevent monopolies, and outlaw price discrimination, to protect employees, consumers, and the environment, to impose various taxes, and to generally provide legal guidelines and limits for all business transactions from the time raw materials are purchased until the finished products or services are delivered to a consumer.

The following specific factors are included in this *government* category:

1. Regulations,
2. Taxes,
3. Programs, and
4. Politics.

These factors should be studied carefully as they specifically apply to the new venture, since failure to comply with the appropriate government requirements can easily result in serious legal problems, perhaps even in termination of the entire venture.

Regulations. Government regulations are, mostly, necessary but aggravating. Regulations imposed by the federal government have three broad functions: (1) to maintain competition, (2) to promote health and safety, and (3) to implement public policy. Federal government regulations can generally be worked with satisfactorily, since they apply to competitors as well, regardless of location. State and local regulations, though, can create either competitive advantages or disadvantages, since competitors located in other areas will be subject to different regulations. The impact of government regulations, then, must be viewed in a competitive sense:

How burdensome are government controls or rulings likely to be?

Answers can be rated as follows:

1 = Current or imminent regulations on zoning, safety, price fixing, monopoly, strategic materials, pollution, or the like will seriously jeopardize operating profitability.

5 = Regulations are not likely to affect the venture.

10 = Current or imminent regulations substantially enhance the venture's outlook.

Factor Weights by Industry Groups — Regulations

Industry Group	Factor Weight	Industry Group	Factor Weight
Agriculture	2	Wholesale and Retail Trade	1
Mining	3	Finance, Insurance, Real Estate	2
Contract Construction	2	Services	1
Manufacturing	1	Government	2
Transportation	2		

Taxes. Taxes will be imposed by every government agency, from federal to neighborhood, that has the authority to do so. The new venture will pay taxes to the federal, state, city, and county governments. Taxes will be paid on what is purchased, what is sold, what is used, and what is left. Taxes will be levied on payrolls, equipment, inventories, and personal property. Tax incentives will also be offered in some cases, either in the form of deductions (through expensing or depreciation) or tax credits. State and local governments may offer substantial tax advantages to encourage the establishment of new businesses within their jurisdictions, especially those with substantial payrolls. In other cases, though, established businesses may hold a competitive advantage over new ventures by virtue of operating under older and lower tax bases. These special tax considerations may have a significant impact on the new business, so ask:

To what extent will special tax considerations affect this venture?

Answers rate on this scale:

  1 = Taxes will severly penalize the venture, compared with competition.

  5 = Taxes are normal compared to competition.

  10 = The company will enjoy substantial tax advantages compared to competition.

Factor Weights by Industry Groups — Taxes

Industry Group	Factor Weight	Industry Group	Factor Weight
Agriculture	2	Wholesale and Retail Trade	1
Mining	2	Finance, Insurance, Real Estate	2
Contract Construction	1	Services	1
Manufacturing	1	Government	3
Transportation	2		

Programs. As government expands, it is continually coming up with new programs that affect the business venture, and many industries and businesses are highly sensitive to how these govenment programs are administered. A substantial portion of the gross national product consists of government expenditures for goods and services, and a large part of federal spending for defense, conservation, transportation, education, health and welfare, environmental protection, and other major programs eventually ends up as sales income for the private sector. Even businesses that are not directly involved with government sales will be indirectly affected by government programs concerning supplies, customers, and employees. The question is:

To what extent will current or imminent government programs affect the venture, either directly or indirectly?

The impact of government programs is rated on this scale:

1 = The trend of governmental programs is sharply reducing market potentials, or is increasing production costs.

5 = No effect whatsoever.

10 = The trend of government programs is sharply expanding the market potential.

Factor Weights by Industry Groups — Programs

Industry Group	Factor Weight	Industry Group	Factor Weight
Agriculture	2	Wholesale and Retail Trade	1
Mining	2	Finance, Insurance, Real Estate	1
Contract Construction	2	Services	2
Manufacturing	1	Government	3
Transportation	2		

Politics. There is no denying the importance of politics in business, since many business decisions are necessarily based on political considerations. Frequently, the greatest politically related difficulties can come from the lowest levels of political influence. A building inspector, for example, can halt the construction or prevent the occupancy of a major project by his own interpretation of building codes, a health or safety inspector can shut down an operating business, and some minor political appointee might reject or make difficult an application for a local building permit or business license.

Good relationships with persons having political influence are obvious advantages for any business, and this is an important question:

How is the political situation expected to influence the venture?

The political climate rates as follows:

1 = Extremely unfavorable.
5 = No effect or influence whatsoever.
10 = Extremely favorable.

Factor Weights by Industry Groups — Politics

Industry Group	Factor Weight	Industry Group	Factor Weight
Agriculture	1	Wholesale and Retail Trade	1
Mining	2	Finance, Insurance, Real Estate	2
Contract Construction	2	Services	2
Manufacturing	1	Government	3
Transportation	2		

Summary of Government Factors. The four government-related factors included in this category aim toward examining how government influences of all types might be expected to affect this specific venture. The questions that need to be answered in this respect are:

1. *Regulations*—how burdensome are government controls or rulings likely to be?
2. *Taxes*—to what extent will special tax considerations affect this venture?
3. *Programs*—to what extent will current or imminent government programs directly or indirectly affect the venture?
4. *Politics*—how is the political situation expected to influence the venture?

SUMMARY OF ENVIRONMENTAL FACTORS

Environmental factors—those factors that are critical to the success of a new venture, but that are beyond the control of the venturing company—constitute the most important major facet in new venture success.

Four important groups of environmental factors make up this category:

1. *Market.* Is there a strong market for this item, considering potential volume, proportion, fertility, growth, stability, and future outlook?
2. *Competition.* What kind of competition dominates this market, in terms of size, specialization, entrenchment, pricing, and possible entry reaction?
3. *Suppliers.* Is the industry well situated for supplies and services with respect to the specific materials, equipment, and services needed, and how dependent is the business upon these suppliers?
4. *Government.* How might government be expected to affect this venture, considering the overall situation with respect to regulations, taxes, programs, and politics?

A SAVE rating sheet, incorporating the 19 factors making up the *environment* category, is shown in Fig. 5-2.

For these environmental factors, the maximum possible scores for the four major factor groups, in each of the nine industry groups, are as follows:

Maximum Possible Score

Industry Group	Market	Competition	Suppliers	Government	Total
Agriculture	70	60	70	70	270
Mining	70	70	50	90	280
Contract Construction	60	70	70	70	270
Manufacturing	60	50	40	40	190
Transportation	60	80	60	80	280
Wholesale and Retail Trade	70	80	60	40	250
Finance, Insurance, Real Estate	60	60	40	70	230
Services	60	80	50	60	250
Government	60	80	40	110	290

Together, these environmental factors account for between 25 and 30 percent of the success of a new business venture. While they cannot be controlled, they can and must be anticipated in the company's strategic plans.

Factor	Factor Rating	Factor Weight	Factor Score	Factor Group	Factor Group Score
Volume	_____	_____	_____		
Proportion	_____	_____	_____		
Fertility	_____	_____	_____	Market	_____
Growth	_____	_____	_____		
Stability	_____	_____	_____		
Outlook	_____	_____	_____		
Size	_____	_____	_____		
Specialization	_____	_____	_____		
Entrenchment	_____	_____	_____	Competition	_____
Pricing	_____	_____	_____		
Entry Reaction	_____	_____	_____		
Materials	_____	_____	_____		
Equipment	_____	_____	_____	Suppliers	_____
Services	_____	_____	_____		
Dependency	_____	_____	_____		
Regulations	_____	_____	_____		
Taxes	_____	_____	_____	Government	_____
Programs	_____	_____	_____		
Politics	_____	_____	_____		

Total Environment Score   _____
Total Score Possible   _____
Environment Efficiency Percentage _____

Fig. 5-2. SAVE rating sheet for environment factors.

6
The Venture

By definition, the term *venture* refers to a speculative business undertaking involving chance, danger, hazard, and/or risk.

A number of factors relating to the venture itself—rather than specifically to the item, the company, or the environment—enter into the final decision regarding a venture's overall attractiveness and suitability, as well as its chances of becoming successful.

In looking at the attractiveness of the proposed business venture as a whole, it is necessary to look at how strongly the venture is supported by those whose participation is essential to its success, at the economic desirability of making the required financial commitments in the venture, and at how well the venture serves the company's interests.

These considerations are covered in the following three factor groups:

1. Support,
2. Investment, and
3. Strategy.

Figure 6-1 illustrates the organization of the 16 venture-related factors contained in these three factor groups.

Together, the factors included in these three venture factor groups will give a broad picture of the venture's attractiveness and appropriateness for the venturing company to offer the proposed item in the existing environment.

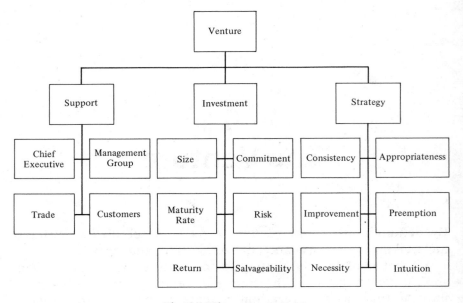

Fig. 6-1. The venture model.

SUPPORT

It is a poor project that cannot generate some enthusiasm from any-one but its originators and immediate sponsors. The total strength with which a new venture is supported—not just by a few individuals, but by everyone upon whose efforts the venture's success or failure will ultimately rest—is an essential ingredient in the venture's successful outcome.

Support for the venture, then, must come from throughout the item's environment, from the company's top management down through the entire distribution chain to the ultimate consumer. In particular, the strength of venture support should be appraised from the following viewpoints, reflected in these specific factors:

1. Chief executive,
2. Management group,
3. Trade, and
4. Customers.

Analysis of these factors will tell if and where support needs to be bolstered to enhance the venture's success potential.

Chief Executive. Enthusiastic support for a new venture by the company's chief executive is one sure way of seeing that the project is at least given a careful evaluation from within the company. A possible danger is that the evaluation might be unrealistically optimistic, aimed at pleasing the chief executive rather than critically assessing the business situation. Nevertheless, support at the top is an important consideration, reflected in this question:

To what extent does the chief executive sponsor the proposal?

Answers rate as follows:
  1 = Very skeptical.
  5 = Actively interested and generally favorable.
  10 = Enthusiastic authorship and full sponsorship.

Factor Weights by Industry Groups — Chief Executive			
Industry Group	Factor Weight	Industry Group	Factor Weight
Agriculture	1	Wholesale and Retail Trade	1
Mining	1	Finance, Insurance, Real Estate	1
Contract Construction	1	Services	1
Manufacturing	1	Government	3
Transportation	1		

Management Group. Support of the company's full operating management group is obviously an important factor, since these managers exercise direct control over most of the individual factors included in the *item* and *company* categories. People in sales are likely to view new projects from an entirely different perspective than those involved in research, production, finance, or other management functions, and there are bound to be some conflicting opinions on almost any proposal. The question is:

Does the operating management group support the proposal?

The answers are scored in this manner:
  1 = Managers most directly responsible are very skeptical.
  5 = Managers most responsible for the venture's success are actively interested and generally favorable.
  10 = Entire management group is highly enthusiastic.

Factor Weights by Industry Groups — Management Group

Industry Group	Factor Weight	Industry Group	Factor Weight
Agriculture	1	Wholesale and Retail Trade	1
Mining	1	Finance, Insurance, Real Estate	1
Contract Construction	1	Services	1
Manufacturing	1	Government	3
Transportation	1		

Trade. The company's key agents, distributors, dealers, and other representatives are critical links in the flow of any item from its source to its ultimate consumers. Any reluctance on their part toward the new item or venture can easily slow down the physical product flow in one direction (producer to consumer) and prevent an open communications flow in the other direction (consumer to producer). If possible, the venture support to be expected from the trade should be determined through direct communication with trade sources. Find out:

To what extent do the company's key agents, distributors, dealers, and other representatives support the proposal?

Trade support is rated as follows:

1 = Very skeptical.

5 = Actively interested, generally favorable.

10 = Have made actual commitments for initial volumes.

Factor Weights by Industry Groups — Trade

Industry Group	Factor Weight	Industry Group	Factor Weight
Agriculture	1	Wholesale and Retail Trade	1
Mining	1	Finance, Insurance, Real Estate	1
Contract Construction	1	Services	1
Manufacturing	1	Government	2
Transportation	1		

Customers. Customers seldom share the enthusiasm for a new venture that is shown by the venture's originators and supporters within the company. Many new businesses have died quickly and quietly for just this reason. It is sometimes difficult for someone who has perhaps originated and worked with, even become totally immersed in, a new venture idea to even imagine that others will not be equally impressed—but chances are, they will not be. Customer support must be earned, not anticipated. Tests have shown that, on the average, only about 30 percent of the customers who *should* be interested in a new product, actually are; of these 30 percent, 10 percent or less will actually buy the product. Ask this question:

To what extent do customers (or key prospects) endorse the venture?

Their level of interest may be rated on this scale:
1 = Very skeptical.
5 = Actively interested, generally favorable.
10 = Have actually issued purchase orders.

Factor Weights by Industry Groups—Customers

Industry Group	Factor Weight	Industry Group	Factor Weight
Agriculture	1	Wholesale and Retail Trade	1
Mining	1	Finance, Insurance, Real Estate	1
Contract Construction	1	Services	1
Manufacturing	1	Government	2
Transportation	1		

Summary of Support Factors. The venture support factors measure how strongly the proposed venture is likely to be supported by those whose support is most needed, both from within and without the company. These four factors measure venture support:

1. *Chief Executive*—to what extent does the chief executive sponsor the proposal?
2. *Management Group*—does the operating management group support the proposal?
3. *Trade*—to what extent do the company's key agents, distributors, dealers, and other representatives support the proposal?
4. *Customers*—to what extent do customers (or key prospects) endorse the venture?

In all cases, the level of interest shown by these individuals or groups is measured on a scale ranging from extreme skepticism to active and enthusiastic involvement.

INVESTMENT

There are many methods available for evaluating capital expenditures, but the only good way to manage investments is to carefully think through the economics of each individual proposal, and make decisions accordingly. There is only a limited amount of time during which a specific business venture (product, process, or service) can remain profitable—until it reaches the "golden years" of its life cycle and begins to suffer declining health.

While investment decisions may be justified on the basis of necessity or payout time, the rate of return on invested capital is the most logical and theoretically acceptable means of determining investment feasibility. Rate of return depends on the magnitude and timing of all cash flows throughout the life of the project, relating anticipated earnings to the amount of capital tied up during the project's estimated life, considering the time value of money.

The SAVE study, though, is (or should be) conducted during the early stages of a proposed new venture, perhaps even before any reliable cost estimates and cash flow projections are possible. Consequently, the factors included in the *investment* category are not designed to provide an analytical procedure for computing venture profitability, but rather to measure the company's affinity for the venture in terms of the anticipated investment. The specific investment-related factors considered here are:

1. Size,
2. Commitment,
3. Maturity rate,
4. Risk,
5. Return, and
6. Salvability.

While these factors are insufficient in themselves to establish a percentage rate of return on invested capital, they can reveal generally whether or not the proposed venture constitutes a good investment opportunity for the company.

Size. The magnitude of the investment required in a new venture can be an overriding consideration. If it is larger than the company can handle, the venture may not be possible as planned, despite its many virtues. Sizable outside capital requirements or the necessity to embark on a joint venture present a whole new set of problems. Ideally, the new venture should commit only a small portion of the company's available financial resources, and any project demanding an investment totaling more than half the company's net worth should be viewed skeptically. Ask this question:

What is the total estimated venture cost as a percentage of the company's net worth?

Score the response as follows:
  1 = 50 percent or more.
  5 = About 15 percent.
  10 = 5 percent or less.

Factor Weights by Industry Groups — Size			
Industry Group	Factor Weight	Industry Group	Factor Weight
Agriculture	1	Wholesale and Retail Trade	1
Mining	2	Finance, Insurance, Real Estate	1
Contract Construction	1	Services	1
Manufacturing	1	Government	1
Transportation	1		

Commitment. Sending good money after bad is to be avoided, but there are cases where enough has already been spent that only a relatively small incremental investment remains to be made to bring a new venture to an operational condition. In such cases, even projects with marginal or unpredictable success potential might be worth completing. On the other hand, if very little has been actually committed, the project can easily be terminated or abandoned without any great penalty. The key question is:

What percentage of the total venture cost has already been committed?

The percentages will fall in these scoring brackets:
  1 = 5 percent or less.
  5 = About 25 percent.
  10 = 50 percent or more.

Factor Weights by Industry Groups — Commitment

Industry Group	Factor Weight	Industry Group	Factor Weight
Agriculture	1	Wholesale and Retail Trade	1
Mining	1	Finance, Insurance, Real Estate	1
Contract Construction	1	Services	1
Manufacturing	1	Government	2
Transportation	1		

Maturity Rate. A certain period of time is necessary to build up any new business to its normal operating level. The cost of supporting the business until it is able to support itself through sales is an important consideration in estimating the total capital requirements. New businesses generally grow in one of two patterns: (1) a relatively slow start-up phase, followed by a period of rapid growth until the business reaches maturity and a more modest growth rate; or (2) a rapid growth period at the beginning, slowing down and leveling off as the business matures. The time scale can vary widely in either case, from several months to many years. The quicker that sales can be brought up to their planned normal level, the more rapidly the company's initial investment can be recovered, and the less economic risk that will be endured. In assessing the maturity rate factor, determine:

How long will it take for sales volume to reach substantially full development?

Maturity times score as follows:

  1 = 9 years or more.
  5 = 5 years.
10 = 1 year or less.

Factor Weights by Industry Groups — Maturity Rate

Industry Group	Factor Weight	Industry Group	Factor Weight
Agriculture	2	Wholesale and Retail Trade	1
Mining	2	Finance, Insurance, Real Estate	1
Contract Construction	3	Services	2
Manufacturing	1	Government	0
Transportation	1		

Risk. There are four different categories of risks inherent in any new business venture: (1) there are risks that *must be taken*, just to be in business; (2) there are risks that *should be taken*, in pursuing opportunities for profit; (3) there are risks that are *too great to take,* usually for economic reasons; and (4) there are risks that are *too good not to take*, where the possibility of very high rewards outweighs the risks involved. The main concern should not be with eliminating risks, but rather in selecting the right risks to be taken. The only way to eliminate risk is to do nothing, which in business is actually the most disastrous risk of all. In evaluating the risk factor for the proposed new venture, ask:

How would you classify the investment risk?

Risks score as follows:

  1 = A pure speculation (50-50 odds or worse).
  5 = A normal business risk (3-1 odds in its favor).
10 = An extremely safe proposition (10-1 odds or better).

Factor Weights by Industry Groups — Risk			
Industry Group	Factor Weight	Industry Group	Factor Weight
Agriculture	2	Wholesale and Retail Trade	1
Mining	3	Finance, Insurance, Real Estate	1
Contract Construction	2	Services	2
Manufacturing	1	Government	0
Transportation	1		

Return. What constitutes a fair rate of return on invested capital varies with the nation's economy, the company's cost of money, and the returns possible on alternative investments of comparable risk. Most established, well-managed companies expect to earn a return of some 15 to 30 percent on their stockholders' equity, and many do better. A new venture should conservatively offer at least a return comparable to the company's other business activities, and should preferably offer a much higher return potential; it should never earn less than the company as a whole. Ask:

What is the estimated annual rate of return on investment over the venture's economic life (using a present value or discounted cash flow basis)?

Use these guidelines to score the answers:

  1 = Very low, less than the company's cost of money.

5 = Medium, about equal to the company's rate of return on total investment.

10 = High, at least double the company's rate of return on its total operations.

	Factor Weights by Industry Groups — Return		
Industry Group	Factor Weight	Industry Group	Factor Weight
Agriculture	1	Wholesale and Retail Trade	1
Mining	1	Finance, Insurance, Real Estate	1
Contract Construction	1	Services	1
Manufacturing	1	Government	1
Transportation	1		

Salvability. Much of the money and effort spent on a new venture will probably go down the tube should the venture fail. Some expenditures on a new project, though, may be for items that can either be used elsewhere in the business, or that can be converted back into cash. The term *salvability* refers to the portion of the total investment in the new venture that can be saved or salvaged if the venture fails. Here, the question is:

If the venture should happen to fail, what portion of the total investment could be salvaged usefully or converted to cash?

Salvability percentages are scored like this:

1 = 10 percent or less; practically a total loss.

5 = About 50 percent; can recover about 50 cents on the dollar.

10 = 90 percent or more of the investment can be recovered or salvaged.

	Factor Weights by Industry Groups — Salvability		
Industry Group	Factor Weight	Industry Group	Factor Weight
Agriculture	1	Wholesale and Retail Trade	2
Mining	2	Finance, Insurance, Real Estate	1
Contract Construction	2	Services	1
Manufacturing	1	Government	1
Transportation	1		

Summary of Investment Factors. The six investment-related factors covered in this section are aimed at determining whether or not the proposed venture constitutes a good investment for the venturing company. These factors cover a wide range of important considerations:

1. *Size*—what is the total venture cost as a percentage of the company's net worth?
2. *Commitment*—what percentage of the total venture cost has already been committed?
3. *Maturity Rate*—how long will it take for sales volume to reach substantially full development?
4. *Risk*—how would you classify the investment risk?
5. *Return*—what is the estimated annual rate of return on investment over the venture's economic life, using a present value or discounted cash flow basis?
6. *Salvability*—if the venture should happen to fail, what portion of the total investment could be salvaged usefully or converted to cash?

STRATEGY

Business strategy can be defined in a number of different ways:

- Skillful management in getting the better of an adversary.
- The means by which a company employs its limited financial and physical resources in accomplishing its objectives.
- The science and art of meeting competition under the most advantageous conditions possible.
- The art of devising and employing plans toward a specified goal.
- Management's ideas regarding the firm's objectives, the means by which these objectives will be accomplished, and the reasons for pursuing them.

In all cases, business strategy involves management's decisions in the face of uncertain competition in the attempt to meet this uncertain competition under the most favorable terms possible in the existing environment. Sound strategy is an essential ingredient for success in every competitive situation, and much of the difference between success and failure in business can be attributed to management's ability to make the strategic decision at the strategic time.

The specific factors included in this venture strategy category are:

1. Consistency,
2. Appropriateness,
3. Improvement,
4. Preemption,
5. Necessity, and
6. Intuition.

The key consideration in evaluating all of these strategic factors is concerned with how well the proposed venture serves the company's overall best interests.

Consistency. A company may develop a reputation for a certain quality of performance in its chosen fields of specialization. This reputation may carry over into new ventures, even before it is earned through performance. Or, conversely, the reputation earned in the new venture—whether good or bad—may carry back over to the company's established business lines. It is therefore important that the new venture be consistent or compatible with the company's basic purposes, planned objectives, near-term intentions, operating policies, public image, and employee, customer, trade, investor, and contract obligations. If the company has maintained a high-quality image, introducing a low-quality item may be a mistake, regardless of the volume it generates. Likewise, a company noted for low-priced items may err in bringing out a high-priced line, except to enhance the image of the company's other products or services. Ask:

To what extent is the venture consistent with the company's goals, policies, obligations, and image?

Rank the answers as follows:
  1 = Very unlike what the company stands for.
  5 = Reasonably consistent with the company's present situation.
  10 = Dramatically enhances and complements what the company stands for.

Factor Weights by Industry Groups—Consistency

Industry Group	Factor Weight	Industry Group	Factor Weight
Agriculture	1	Wholesale and Retail Trade	1
Mining	1	Finance, Insurance, Real Estate	2
Contract Construction	1	Services	2
Manufacturing	1	Government	2
Transportation	1		

Appropriateness. Some ventures are obviously especially well suited to a particular company, while others are noticeably inappropriate or untimely. The suitability of the proposed venture should be considered in light of the company's size, traditions, location, marketing operations and know-how, production operations and know-how, technical and managerial know-how, and prospective markets. The question to be asked is:

How appropriate is this venture as a company undertaking?

Appropriateness is rated on this scale:
1 = Flatly inappropriate.
5 = Reasonably appropriate.
10 = A perfect fit.

Factor Weights by Industry Groups—Appropriateness

Industry Group	Factor Weight	Industry Group	Factor Weight
Agriculture	1	Wholesale and Retail Trade	1
Mining	1	Finance, Insurance, Real Estate	2
Contract Construction	1	Services	1
Manufacturing	1	Government	2
Transportation	1		

Improvement. It must be recognized that any major new venture will have some effect on many of the company's other activities; hopefully, it will improve the company's position with respect to these other interests. Some of the factors that might be influenced one way or another by the new venture include:

investors   taxes
services   competitors

suppliers
purchasing power
agents or representatives
distributors
dealers
managerial efficiency
product line
customers
unions
key employees
public relations

economies of scale
defensive posture
offensive posture
captive sales
reciprocity sales
repeat sales
facilities utilization
technology utilization
capital utilization
marketing efficiency
synergism

With respect to these various factors and considerations, ask the following question:

To what extent will this venture improve the company and strengthen its overall position?

Answers rate on this scale:

1 = Substantially weakens the company's position.
5 = Significantly improves several important areas.
10 = Tremendously improves, and is badly needed, in many important areas.

Factor Weights by Industry Groups—Improvement			
Industry Group	Factor Weight	Industry Group	Factor Weight
Agriculture	1	Wholesale and Retail Trade	1
Mining	1	Finance, Insurance, Real Estate	1
Contract Construction	1	Services	1
Manufacturing	1	Government	3
Transportation	1		

Preemption. At any given time, a company is likely to have a number of different investment opportunities available to it, one or more of which may appear to offer considerable promise and good strategic value. At the same time, the company's resources are limited in terms of money, management, personnel, technology, capacity, or any number of other critical factors, and a single choice must be made. Also, in addition to limited resources, there may be compelling legal, competitive, or other reasons why engaging in certain ventures might preclude the possibility of engaging in other, perhaps equally attractive, ventures. The question is:

To what extent would pursuit of this venture preempt other promising opportunities which are open to the company?

Answers are rated as follows:

1 = Venture would permanently eliminate several opportunities which appear to have considerable promise and strategic value.

5 = Venture would cause important postponements but no permanent losses among other promising proposals.

10 = Venture would not cause important losses or postponements: company urgently needs certain new opportunities created by the venture itself.

Factor Weights by Industry Groups — Preemption

Industry Group	Factor Weight	Industry Group	Factor Weight
Agriculture	1	Wholesale and Retail Trade	1
Mining	2	Finance, Insurance, Real Estate	1
Contract Construction	2	Services	2
Manufacturing	1	Government	2
Transportation	1		

Necessity. Business ventures entered into out of necessity include many of the investments that an investor would rather not make, but must. Typically included in the necessary category are: replacement of worn out, broken-down, antiquated, or otherwise unsuitable facilities or equipment, programs required to comply with governmental regulations, and new ventures that, even though relatively unprofitable, are necessary to meet competition. Ventures based on necessity, while not necessarily profitable, are usually preferable to any available alternatives. It is difficult to appraise these ventures, since there is no real objective means of measuring necessity. Nevertheless, ask:

To what extent is this venture really necessary for the company?

Degree of necessity will fall somewhere on this scale:

1 = It is purely optional.

5 = It is a mild but real need.

10 = It is an absolute necessity.

Factor Weights by Industry Groups—Necessity			
Industry Group	Factor Weight	Industry Group	Factor Weight
Agriculture	1	Wholesale and Retail Trade	2
Mining	1	Finance, Insurance, Real Estate	2
Contract Construction	1	Services	2
Manufacturing	1	Government	3
Transportation	2		

Intuition. Intuition is knowledge obtained without recourse to inference or reasoning, involving a quick or ready apprehension or subconscious feeling about an idea, and does not provide a good basis for running a business or evaluating a new venture—but it does have its place. Intuitive feelings or hunches are not always formed without some basis in fact or some experience lurking in the evaluator's background, and such feelings should not be ignored. Some businesses have, in fact, succeeded largely because their management was able to make quick correct intuitive decisions. Ask this question:

Intuitively, how do you feel about the overall chances of success for the proposed venture?

Rank these intuitive feelings on this scale:

1 = Fearful, negative.

5 = No intuitive feeling at all.

10 = Buoyantly confident.

Factor Weights by Industry Groups—Intuition			
Industry Group	Factor Weight	Industry Group	Factor Weight
Agriculture	1	Wholesale and Retail Trade	2
Mining	1	Finance, Insurance, Real Estate	1
Contract Construction	2	Services	2
Manufacturing	1	Government	2
Transportation	1		

Summary of Strategy Factors. The venture strategy factors attempt to define how well the proposed venture can be expected to serve the company's overall best interests. The six strategic factors cover the following points:

1. *Consistency*—to what extent is the venture consistent with the company's goals, policies, obligations, and image?
2. *Appropriateness*—how appropriate is this venture as a company undertaking?
3. *Improvement*—to what extent will this venture improve the company and strengthen its overall position?
4. *Preemption*—to what extent would pursuit of this venture preempt other promising opportunities which are open to the company?
5. *Necessity*—to what extent is this venture really necessary for the company?
6. *Intuition*—intuitively, how do you feel about the overall chances of success for the proposed venture?

SUMMARY OF VENTURE FACTORS

Sixteen specific factors are included among the venture-related considerations, divided among three major factor groups. The purpose of the venture category is to measure the general attractiveness of the proposed venture, for the particular company, in the existing environment.

The venture factors can be summarized as follows:

1. *Support.* How strongly supported is the venture by the company's chief executive and operating managers, as well as by the trade and important customers or key prospects?
2. *Investment.* Is the proposed venture a good investment, considering such factors as size, commitment, maturity rate, risk, return, and salvability?
3. *Strategy.* How well does the proposed venture serve the company's overall interests, measured in terms of its consistency, appropriateness, improvement potential, preemption considerations, necessity, and intuitively judged success potential?

A SAVE rating sheet, incorporating all 16 of the venture factors, is shown in Fig. 6-2.

Factor	Factor Rating	Factor Weight	Factor Score	Factor Group	Factor Group Score
Chief Executive	_____	_____	_____		
Management Group	_____	_____	_____	Support	_____
Trade	_____	_____	_____		
Customers	_____	_____	_____		
Size	_____	_____	_____		
Commitment	_____	_____	_____		
Maturity Rate	_____	_____	_____	Investment	_____
Risk	_____	_____	_____		
Return	_____	_____	_____		
Salvability	_____	_____	_____		
Consistency	_____	_____	_____		
Appropriateness	_____	_____	_____		
Improvement	_____	_____	_____	Strategy	_____
Preemption	_____	_____	_____		
Necessity	_____	_____	_____		
Intuition	_____	_____	_____		
Total Venture Score					_____
Total Score Possible					_____
Venture Efficiency Percentage					_____

Fig. 6-2. SAVE rating sheet for venture factors.

The maximum scores possible for the various venture factors, based on the weights assigned to the different industry groups, are as follows:

Maximum Possible Score

Industry Group	Support	Invest-ment	Strategy	Total
Agriculture	40	80	60	180
Mining	40	110	70	220
Contract Construction	40	100	80	220
Manufacturing	40	60	60	160
Transportation	40	60	70	170
Wholesale and Retail Trade	40	70	80	190
Finance, Insurance, Real Estate	40	60	90	190
Services	40	80	100	220
Government	100	50	140	290

Factors relating to the venture itself rather than to the item, company, or environment, together account for between 20 and 25 percent of the success potential of a new business venture. As with the other major aspects, any serious deficiencies that cannot be corrected must cast doubt on the entire venture.

7
The Chances For Success

Simply recognizing, thinking about, and mentally evaluating the 69 SAVE factors in an organized and structured way will greatly enhance the evaluator's perception and understanding of the new venture's four major aspects: (1) the *item* to be sold, whether it is a product, a service, or any other type of project, (2) the *company* (or *venturer*) who plans to sell the item, (3) the *environment* in which it must be sold, and (4) certain important aspects of the *venture* itself.

Briefly summarizing the four major aspects which ultimately determine the success or failure of any new business venture:

1. *The item*—how good is this item in terms of its performance, salability, and defensibility?
2. *The company*—can the company handle it well, considering its marketing, technical, and production capabilities?

or

The venturer—does he have the capabilities required for this enterprise, as evidenced by his personal traits, know-how, and other strengths?
3. *The environment*—how favorable is the environment for this venture, measured in terms of market, competitive, supply, and government factors?
4. *The venture*—how attractive is the venture for this company, in view of its internal and external support, investment requirements, and strategic considerations?

The success of any new business venture rests upon both strength and balance in these four major aspects, and upon the 69 specific factors of which they are composed.

A project, for example, that achieves nearly perfect ratings in three of the major aspects but that is rated very poorly in the fourth cannot be said to have a high overall rating; such imbalance will simply not support a successful business venture. The outstanding product with no market, or even with a strong market but a company without marketing capabilities, will not be successful unless the deficiencies can be overcome; nor is an inferior product or service likely to make it in the marketplace, regardless of the size of the potential market or the marketing abilities of the venturing company. Balance, as well as strength, is absolutely essential.

THE CAPACITY FOR SUCCESS

SAVE—Strategic Analysis for Venture Evaluation—was developed to provide an improved method of appraising proposed new business ventures of all types to determine the extent to which they merit the interest and support of the venturing company or the individual venturer.

Most conventional evaluation procedures confine their attention to the financial aspects of an enterprise, and they are almost entirely concerned with measuring the venture's capacity for failure. Such approaches tend to ignore or undervalue many factors which may actually contribute more toward venture success than good financial strength. The problem is especially critical in assessing new businesses, where capitalization is frequently so weak that the proposed venture may be rejected almost automatically by conventional evaluation standards.

It is not enough—and is, in fact, dangerous—to simply relax the obligations of financial prudence to accommodate such situations. It is necessary instead to gauge the proposed venture's capacity for success by measuring all of the factors which influence that success.

The SAVE approach attempts to do this in practical and consistent terms, in a format which facilitates quick screening as well as thorough analysis. It provides ratings which are comparable, as between different types of ventures, or between different points in time, or even between preliminary and final evaluations.

The SAVE approach assumes that a competent evaluator generally has adequate knowledge to enable him to make useful assessments of a proposed venture's merits at any given point in time.

His assessments need not be perfectly accurate or completely knowledgeable in order to be useful. The idea is simply to make the fullest possible use of what he does know. Obviously, part of the usefulness of such assessments is the specific identification of areas where more knowledge is needed, but it has been proven in an astonishing number of instances that present knowledge is quite sufficient for early-stage evaluations.

With conventional techniques, it often happens that more is known about a venture than can be used effectively to evaluate it; this is because the techniques are not comprehensive or functional beyond the financial sector. The result is wasted knowledge in certain areas and unidentified blind spots in other areas.

SAVE, though, forces the evaluator to look at all four faces of any proposed new venture: the item involved in the venture (product, service, or other), the capabilities of the venturer or venturing company, the environment in which it will exist, and the overall venture itself.

FACTORS AFFECTING SUCCESS

Success in any business requires that a great many things be done right, and that very few things be done wrong.

The 69 factors included in the SAVE approach are all important contributors to the success of a new or existing business venture. If the existing venture is already successful, then all, or at least most, of these 69 factors have already been integrated in the enterprise—if not intentionally, intuitively. If the venture in question is still in the proposal or planning stage, then at least the necessary factors are known in advance.

The relative importance of the 69 individual factors, 13 factor groups, and four major aspects incorporated in the SAVE approach will vary from industry to industry and from company to company. In the manufacturing industry, for example, each of the 69 factors is weighted at one; this simply assigns equal importance to each.

In other industries, some factors will assume greater importance than others, and are therefore weighted differently. In a retail business, convenience and tradability are especially important; the agricultural, mining, and construction fields are highly technique-oriented; government projects are obviously very sensitive to political considerations. The relevant factors are weighted accordingly. On the other hand, a few factors are totally insignificant in certain industries, and are disregarded in those few instances.

Table 7-1 shows the relative significance of the four major aspects—item, company, environment, and venture—in nine selected industry groups.

Table 7-1. Relative importance of major aspects in various industries.

Percentage Weight by Major Aspect

Industry Group	Item	Company	Environment	Venture	Total
Agriculture	22.2	27.8	30.0	20.0	100.0
Mining	21.0	28.4	27.4	23.2	100.0
Contract Construction	18.7	27.4	29.7	24.2	100.0
Manufacturing	20.3	29.0	27.5	23.2	100.0
Transportation	25.8	25.8	30.1	18.3	100.0
Wholesale and Retail Trade	25.0	27.2	27.2	20.6	100.0
Finance, Insurance, Real Estate	22.0	26.8	28.0	23.2	100.0
Services	22.4	28.7	26.6	22.3	100.0
Government	18.4	25.2	28.2	28.2	100.0

It can be seen that the company's capabilities constitute the most important single aspect of venture success in four of the nine industry groups, while environment-related considerations are the most important in the other industries. It is also interesting to note that the item (the product, service, or whatever is being sold) is *never* the most important aspect and is, in fact, in several fields the *least* important.

Disregarding the differences between industry groups, the overall importance of the 13 major factor groups to the success of either an existing or new venture, rank as follows:

Rank	Major Aspect	Factor Group	Percentage Contribution to Venture Success
1	Company	Marketing	11.8
2	Item	Salability	10.6
3	Company	Production	9.3
4	Venture	Strategy	9.2
5	Venture	Investment	8.3
6	Environment	Competition	7.8
7	Environment	Government	7.8

Rank	Major Aspect	Factor Group	Percentage Contribution to Venture Success
8	Environment	Market	7.0
9	Item	Performance	6.2
10	Company	Technology	6.0
11	Environment	Suppliers	5.9
12	Venture	Support	5.2
13	Item	Defensibility	4.9
	Total		100.0

It is especially interesting to note where item performance ranks (ninth) and its contribution to venture success (6.2 percent). Contrary to the "better mousetrap" theory, an outstanding product does not assure success without a lot of assistance in other areas.

This composite list does not apply to any particular industry, since it is based on an average of the nine industries for which factor weights were presented. However, a similar list, easily compiled and applied to a specific field of interest, could provide some useful insights and should greatly improve the evaluator's sense of perception when looking at possible new ventures.

PRELIMINARY SCREENING PROCEDURE

A quick or preliminary screening evaluation is accomplished by scoring or rating a proposed venture anywhere on a scale of 1 to 10 in each of 13 major factor groups, using the SAVE Preliminary Screening Analysis form shown in Fig. 7-1.

The 13 factor groups to be rated have been covered in detail in Chapters 3 to 6. Briefly summarizing the major thrust of each factor group:

- *Performance*—how well does it work?
- *Salability*—how well will it sell?
- *Defensibility*—to what extent can it be defended against direct competition?
- *Marketing*—how effectively can the company market the item?
- *Technical*—how good is the company's technical know-how?
- *Production*—can the company produce the item competitively?
- *Market*—is there a good market for the proposed item?
- *Competition*—how does the company compare with the competition to be encountered?

Factor Group	1 to 10 Rating	Factor Group Weight	Weighted Factor Group Score	Weighted Major Aspect Score	Maximum Possible Score	Efficiency Percentage
Performance	___	___	___ ⎫			
Salability	___	___	___ ⎬ ___	Item	___	___
Defensibility	___	___	___ ⎭			
Marketing	___	___	___ ⎫			
Technology	___	___	___ ⎬ ___	Company	___	___
Production	___	___	___ ⎭			
Market	___	___	___ ⎫			
Competition	___	___	___ ⎪ ___			
Suppliers	___	___	___ ⎨ Environment	___	___	
Government	___	___	___ ⎭			
Support	___	___	___ ⎫			
Investment	___	___	___ ⎬ ___	Venture	___	___
Strategy	___	___	___ ⎭			
Total Screening Rating			___		___	___

Fig. 7-1. SAVE preliminary screening analysis form.

- *Suppliers*—is the industry well situated for supplies and services?
- *Government*—how might government be expected to affect this venture?
- *Support*—how strongly supported is this venture?
- *Investment*—is this a good investment?
- *Strategy*—how well does the proposed venture serve the company's overall interests?

In scoring the various factor groups on a 1 to 10 basis, a score of one indicates an extremely unfavorable condition in relation to a stated norm. A score of five usually represents equality with competition, basic adequacy, or an average position with reference to some stated norm. A ten rating indicates clear-cut industry· leadership, overwhelming advantages over competition, and "world-beater" or "best-possible" connotations. Any number from 1 to 10 may be used to represent the evaluator's judgment on any rating.

Each factor group rating is entered in the appropriate space on the analysis sheet and multiplied by the factor group weight, which depends on the industry in which the venture is classified. Table 7-2 gives the factor group weights for selected industry groups. These weights represent the combined total of the individual factor weights in each factor group, as shown in the earlier chapters.

Next, the weighted factor group scores (the group rating score times the weighting factor) are added together to get the weighted major aspect scores for the item, company, environment, and venture. The maximum possible score for each major aspect amounts to ten times the sum of the factor group weights making up that major aspect. The efficiency percentages can then be calculated, dividing the weighted major aspect score by the maximum possible score. Finally, the total screening rating is found by adding together the four major aspect scores and dividing that total by the sum of the four maximum possible scores, giving the overall efficiency percentage for the total venture. Figure 7-2 shows a completed preliminary screening analysis form for a new venture in the manufacturing industry.

In this example, the proposed venture shows efficiency percentages of 70.7 for the item, 64.0 for the company, 54.7 for the environment, and 67.5 for the venture. The combined totals result in an overall total venture efficiency percentage of 63.6. These figures indicate good general strength and fairly good balance, with the only major deficiency noted in the environment category (but still at an acceptable level). The investment factor shows a weakness typical of a small company attempting a relatively large new venture.

As a general rule of thumb, the following minimum values are suggested for the factor group ratings, the major aspect efficiency percentages, and the total screening rating:

- Individual factor groups—rating of 3.
- Major aspects—efficiency percentage of 40.
- Total screening rating—efficiency percentage of 50.

These are not intended to be absolute limits, but should be regarded as real danger points in most cases. When ratings fall below one or more of these minimum levels, the venture will probably be in trouble unless the weaknesses are either eliminated or well compensated elsewhere.

Table 7-2. Factor group weights for selected industries
Industry Group

Factor Category	Agriculture	Mining	Contract Construction	Manufacturing	Transportation	Wholesale and Retail Trade	Finance, Insurance, Real Estate	Services	Government
Performance	5	6	5	4	6	7	6	6	5
Salability	11	7	9	7	12	11	8	11	10
Defensibility	4	7	3	3	6	5	4	4	4
Marketing	9	9	11	9	10	11	11	13	13
Technology	7	9	6	4	5	4	4	5	5
Production	9	9	8	7	8	10	7	9	8
Market	7	7	6	6	6	7	6	6	6
Competition	6	7	7	5	8	8	6	8	8
Suppliers	7	5	7	4	6	6	4	5	4
Government	7	9	7	4	8	4	7	6	11
Support	4	4	4	4	4	4	4	4	10
Investment	8	11	10	6	6	7	6	8	5
Strategy	6	7	8	6	7	8	9	10	14
Total	90	97	91	69	92	92	82	95	103

Factor Group	1 to 10 Rating ×	Factor Group Weight =	Weighted Factor Group Score	Weighted Major Aspect Score	Maximum Possible Score	Efficiency Percentage
Performance	8	4	32			
Salability	7	7	49	99	140	70.7
Defensibility	6	3	18	Item		
Marketing	6	9	54			
Technology	8	4	32	128	200	64.0
Production	6	7	42	Company		
Market	5	6	30			
Competition	6	5	30	104	190	54.7
Suppliers	6	4	24	Environ-		
Government	5	4	20	ment		
Support	9	4	36			
Investment	4	6	24	108	160	67.5
Strategy	8	6	48	Venture		
Total Screening Rating				439	690	63.6

Fig. 7-2. Example of preliminary screening analysis.

Note that the minimum ratings become progressively higher as the categories are grouped. This is because a venture can usually stand to have some weaknesses if they are sufficiently isolated. But, if severe weakness extends uncompensated throughout a whole broad area of evaluation, then the venture probably has no chance at all. The reason, of course, is that too much of the venture's energies and resources will be used up in trying to repair or shore up the weaknesses, and there will not be enough left for balanced development of the business.

FULL EVALUATION PROCEDURE

Ventures passing the preliminary screening phase will merit a more thorough examination, employing the full SAVE evaluation procedure: analyzing and evaluating the venture in terms of each of the 69 individual factors which can affect its success.

The complete SAVE evaluation proceeds in exactly the same manner as the preliminary screening, except that attention is directed toward more specific elements and more detailed frames of reference. Ratings still range from 1 to 10. Figure 7-3 shows the format used in the complete evaluation procedure.

Each of the 69 factors shown on the rating sheet were discussed in preceding chapters. Also, the appropriate weighting factors to be applied to each factor, depending on the industry classification being considered for the new venture, were covered with the discussion of each factor.

This 69-factor rating sheet provides for three separate ratings of each factor. These ratings may reflect the views of three different people, or they may consist of a high, low, and median estimate for each factor. The weighted scores for each factor should be entered on the rating sheet, then totaled for the various factor groups and major aspects. The results, by factor groups, can then be transferred to the summary sheet shown in Fig. 7-4, compared with the maximum possible scores (computed as before), and expressed in terms of efficiency percentages.

Again as a general guideline or rule of thumb, a minimum rating of 3 for a single factor and efficiency percentages of 40 for a factor group, of 50 for each of the four major facets, and of 60 for the project as a whole, are realistic and workable standards. As mentioned before, a few scattered lower values can be tolerated, if sufficient strengths are shown consistently throughout the venture to compensate for the weaknesses.

Figure 7-5 shows a completed analysis for a proposed new business. This particular business is a small retail and mail-order book store, to be located in a small-town suburb of a major metropolitan area. The store is to specialize in books on certain subjects, for which a specific market can be identified. The individuals involved in the new enterprise have owned and operated a big-city, full-line book store for a number of years.

The three values shown on the rating sheet represent a consensus opinion of the owners, using their most optimistic, most pessimistic, and most likely estimates. The 1 to 10 rating for each factor was weighted according to the factors given earlier for the wholesale and retail trade industry classification. For this industry group, the 69 factors have a maximum possible weighted score of 920. After the weighted raw scores were tabulated as shown in Fig. 7-5, their totals were transferred to the summary sheets shown in Figs. 7-6, 7-7, and

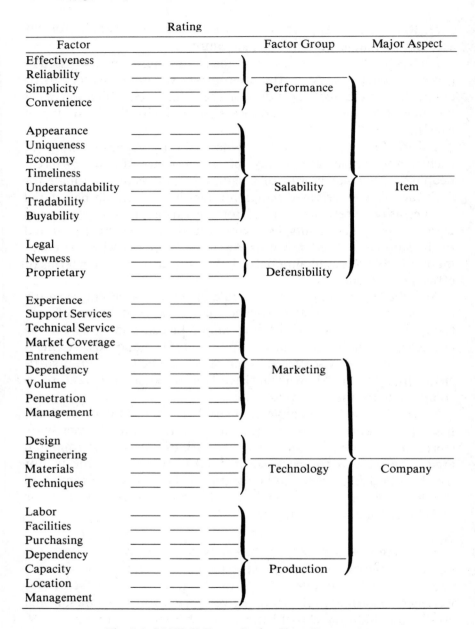

Fig. 7-3. SAVE 69-Factor Rating Sheet (Page 1 of 2)

SAVE 69-Factor Rating Sheet (Page 2 of 2)

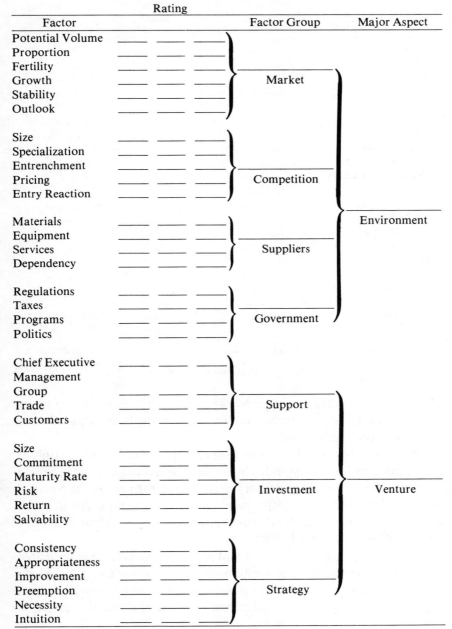

Factor	Rating	Factor Group	Major Aspect
Potential Volume			
Proportion			
Fertility		Market	
Growth			
Stability			
Outlook			
Size			
Specialization			
Entrenchment		Competition	
Pricing			Environment
Entry Reaction			
Materials			
Equipment		Suppliers	
Services			
Dependency			
Regulations			
Taxes		Government	
Programs			
Politics			
Chief Executive			
Management			
Group		Support	
Trade			
Customers			
Size			
Commitment			
Maturity Rate			
Risk		Investment	Venture
Return			
Salvability			
Consistency			
Appropriateness			
Improvement			
Preemption		Strategy	
Necessity			
Intuition			

Fig. 7-3. (continued)

Factor Group	Maximum Possible Score	Actual Score	Efficiency Percentage
Item Factors			
Performance	_____	_____	_____
Salability	_____	_____	_____
Defensibility	_____	_____	_____
Total	_____	_____	_____
Company Factors			
Marketing	_____	_____	_____
Technology	_____	_____	_____
Production	_____	_____	_____
Total	_____	_____	_____
Environmental Factors			
Market	_____	_____	_____
Competition	_____	_____	_____
Suppliers	_____	_____	_____
Government	_____	_____	_____
Total	_____	_____	_____
Venture Factors			
Support	_____	_____	_____
Investment	_____	_____	_____
Strategy	_____	_____	_____
Total	_____	_____	_____
Total Venture	_____	_____	_____

Fig. 7-4. SAVE summary sheet.

7-8. In this way, efficiency percentages could be calculated to cover the entire range of anticipated conditions, from the best possible to the worst imaginable situations.

What is lacking in this, or any other, example of a SAVE study is a full appreciation of the thought processes that the evaluators must go through in assigning the subjective value ratings to the various factors. This procedure simply must actually be performed in order to fully realize how much information, knowledge, and understanding is involved in the evaluation.

In the example, good strength and exceptional balance is indicated by the efficiency percentages exhibited in the four major aspects. As is the case with many new ventures, the environment-related factors over which the company has no control pose the greatest question

Factor	Best	Most Likely	Worst	Factor Group	Major Aspect
Effectiveness	8	7	5		
Reliability	16	14	10	58 51 38	
Simplicity	7	6	5	Performance	
Convenience	27	24	18		
Appearance	6	6	5		
Uniqueness	8	7	5		
Economy	7	5	4		
Timeliness	7	6	3	82 71 50	169 149 107
Understandability	14	12	10	Salability	Item
Tradability	24	21	15		
Buyability	16	14	8		
Legal	6	6	4		
Newness	5	5	5	29 27 19	
Proprietary	18	16	10	Defensibility	
Experience	18	14	12		
Support Services	8	6	5		
Technical Service	5	5	5		
Market Coverage	7	4	2		
Entrenchment	16	12	8	81 64 51	
Dependency	10	10	10	Marketing	
Volume	3	2	1		
Penetration	4	2	1		
Management	10	9	7		
Design	9	7	5		
Engineering	8	6	5	34 28 19	201 168 132
Materials	9	8	5	Technology	Company
Techniques	8	7	4		
Labor	9	9	8		
Facilities	10	9	9		
Purchasing	14	10	10		
Dependency	9	8	6	86 76 62	
Capacity	10	8	5	Production	
Location	16	14	10		
Management	18	18	14		

Fig. 7-5. Example of 69-factor SAVE analysis.
SAVE 69-Factor Rating Sheet (Page 1 of 2)

Factors	Best	Rating Most Likely	Worst	Factor Groups	Major Aspects
Potential Volume	10	9	5		
Proportion	10	10	5		
Fertility	5	4	2	58 46 27	
Growth	9	7	4	Market	
Stability	16	10	8		
Outlook	8	6	3		
Size	12	10	6		
Specialization	16	14	10		
Entrenchment	6	5	4	62 57 37	
Pricing	18	18	12	Competition	
Entry Reaction	10	10	5		
					191 169 102
Materials	14	12	6		Environment
Equipment	10	10	7	50 47 27	
Services	20	20	10	Suppliers	
Dependency	6	5	4		
Regulations	5	5	2		
Taxes	5	5	5	21 19 11	
Programs	6	5	2	Government	
Politics	5	4	2		
Chief Executive	10	10	10		
Management Group	10	10	10	35 33 28	
Trade	6	5	3	Support	
Customers	9	8	5		
Size	7	6	6		
Commitment	9	9	9		
Maturity Rate	9	8	4	54 45 34	151 135 108
Risk	7	5	3	Investment	Venture
Return	6	5	2		
Salvability	16	12	10		
Consistency	10	10	10		
Appropriateness	10	10	9		
Improvement	8	6	5	62 57 46	
Preemption	10	9	8	Strategy	
Necessity	8	8	4		
Intuition	16	14	10		

Fig. 7-5. SAVE 69-Factor Rating Sheet (Page 2 of 2)

Factor Group	Maximum Possible Score	Actual Score	Efficiency Percentage
Item Factors			
Performance	70	58	82.9
Salability	110	82	74.5
Defensibility	50	29	58.0
Total	230	169	73.5
Company Factors			
Marketing	110	81	73.6
Technology	40	34	85.0
Production	100	86	86.0
Total	250	201	80.4
Environment Factors			
Market	70	58	82.9
Competition	80	62	77.5
Suppliers	60	50	83.3
Government	40	21	52.5
Total	250	191	76.4
Venture Factors			
Support	40	35	87.5
Investment	70	54	77.1
Strategy	80	62	77.5
Total	190	151	79.5
Total Venture	920	712	77.4

Fig. 7-6. Example of SAVE summary.
("best" estimate)

mark. In this case the environment-related factors represent a possible threat to the venture's success should the most pessimistic conditions be encountered.

Expressing the evaluation results in terms of a range of estimates, rather than as a single figure, helps considerably in clarifying the situation. The range can be determined as in the example—simply an individual or consensus opinion of the expected range of conditions—or by taking the high, low, and middle value ratings assigned to each factor by several different individuals. Either way, the information is useful.

This identified range of possible conditions, whether established by several estimates from one person or by one estimate from each of several persons, can be used to calculate an *expected value* for the

Factor Group	Maximum Possible Score	Actual Score	Efficiency Percentage
Item Factors			
Performance	70	51	72.9
Salability	110	71	64.5
Defensibility	50	27	54.0
Total	230	149	64.8
Company Factors			
Marketing	110	64	58.2
Technology	40	28	70.0
Production	100	76	76.0
Total	250	168	67.2
Environment Factors			
Market	70	46	65.7
Competition	80	57	71.3
Suppliers	60	47	78.3
Government	40	19	47.5
Total	250	169	67.6
Venture Factors			
Support	40	33	82.5
Investment	70	45	64.3
Strategy	80	57	71.3
Total	190	135	71.1
Total Venture	920	621	67.5

Fig. 7-7. Example of SAVE summary.
("most likely" estimate)

proposed venture, or to compute the *variance* of the separate estimates as a measure of their reliability.

Expected Value. The three estimates developed for the optimistic, pessimistic, and most likely values can be used to calculate a single "expected" value from the formula

$$E = \frac{H + 4M + L}{6}$$

where E is the expected value, H is the high estimate, L is the low estimate, and M is the middle, median, mean, or most likely estimate.

Factor Group	Maximum Possible Score	Actual Score	Efficiency Percentage
Item Factors			
Performance	70	38	54.3
Salability	110	50	45.5
Defensibility	50	19	38.0
Total	230	107	46.5
Company Factors			
Marketing	110	51	46.4
Technology	40	19	47.5
Production	100	62	62.0
Total	250	132	52.8
Environment Factors			
Market	70	27	38.6
Competition	80	37	46.3
Suppliers	60	27	45.0
Government	40	11	27.5
Total	250	102	40.8
Venture Factors			
Support	40	28	70.0
Investment	70	34	48.6
Strategy	80	46	57.5
Total	190	108	56.8
Total Venture	920	449	48.8

Fig. 7-8. Example of SAVE summary.
("worst" estimate)

In the preceding example, where efficiency percentages of 77.4, 67.5, and 48.8 were estimated, the expected value would be

$$E = \frac{77.4 + (4 \times 67.5) + 48.8}{6} = 66.0$$

The same approach can be used for individual factors or factor groups whenever a single value is needed from a group of data.

Variance. Variance is a statistical term commonly used as an indication of the reliability of estimates. If the variance is high, the degree of uncertainty associated with the project is high; a low variance presumably reflects a higher level of confidence in the estimate. Variance (V) is a function of the extreme values—the high and low estimates—and can be calculated from this formula

$$V = \left(\frac{H - L}{6}\right)^2$$

In the example, the variance would be

$$V = \left(\frac{77.4 - 48.8}{6}\right)^2 = 22.7$$

The resulting figure has little significance by itself, but can be used to compare the estimates associated with different ventures being analyzed.

PREDICTING SUCCESS

New ventures sponsored by established companies offer the best opportunities for an accurate prediction of venture success.

In conducting the SAVE analysis in such cases, either the 13-factor preliminary screening technique or the 69-factor comprehensive analysis can be employed. One or more of the company's existing ventures is first evaluated to provide a basis for comparison and for interpreting the results of a similar evaluation of the proposed new venture. Research has shown that the venture results are closely proportional to the overall SAVE ratings.

For example, if an existing project is analyzed and found to have an overall efficiency rating of 60 percent, then a proposed venture with a projected rating of 70 percent will be expected to achieve results 16.7 percent better than the existing project. Or, of two proposed ventures scoring 60 percent and 70 percent efficiency, the second offers 16.7 percent greater potential for success than the first.

The main value of the SAVE approach, then, is as an objective comparative measure of the relative merits of two or more projects, of which—preferably—one has results that are already known.

A 50 percent overall venture efficiency rating indicates simply that the venture is, on the average, about equal to competition in that field. It should, therefore, be about as successful as its average competitors, whatever degree of success this might imply.

The efficiency percentage of a venture is intended to reflect only its relative competitive strength, compared either with competitors, with other ventures having known results, or with other proposed ventures evaluated on the same basis. The SAVE rating indicates that, of several projects comparably evaluated, their relative chances and degrees of success are proportional to their rating scores. The SAVE rating is not intended, by itself, to predict the probability of success for a single venture.

Even with this limitation, though, a single rating score for a single new venture offers the venturing company or individual some meaningful information in attempting to figure the odds of success. The probability of venture success, while not arithmetically the same as the venture's efficiency percentage, is certainly related to that figure.

Just as a firm's production capabilities are limited by whatever necessary resource is in shortest supply, its success capability is limited by whatever factor necessary for success is weakest. For example, the success potential of a firm without a marketing capability is limited by its lack of a marketing capability, despite whatever strengths it possesses in other critical areas.

This leads to what might be termed the *chain theory* of predicting success. Just as a chain is only as strong as its weakest link, or a chair as strong as its weakest leg, the new business venture might be said to be only as strong as its weakest major aspect—whether item, company, environment, or venture. This approach makes some sense.

There is also some credibility to the *cable theory*. Although a chain is only as strong as its weakest link, a cable is stronger than its weakest strand. Strength in other areas can support the weak element.

Recognizing that many people have drowned in ponds that averaged only a few feet deep, the arithmetic mean (or average) is still a statistically sound way of summarizing and expressing arithmetic data.

If a single, specific figure for the probability of success of a proposed new venture is needed, and if there is no objective basis for comparison with other ventures, then the success probability can be assumed to lie somewhere between the "chain" and "cable" values—that is, between the overall venture rating (efficiency percentage) as a maximum, and the lowest of the four major aspect ratings as a minimum.

THE BENEFITS OF SAVE

The SAVE approach promises several potential benefits for companies and individuals who use it as a regular part of their new project screening and evaluation program.

SAVE brings a sophisticated and orderly venture evaluation capability within the economic means of many enterprises which cannot afford conventional project research in this field. Its versatility in being able to handle screening, preliminary evaluations, and in-depth analyses, provides an inexpensive means for exploring the venture horizon much more broadly and meaningfully than has been possible heretofore.

SAVE provides a sound and consistent basis for comparing the merits of various proposals with each other and with present output. It also provides a basis for measuring improvement or deterioration in the merits of a given proposal at different points in time. Hopefully, SAVE will help firms to overcome the "re-rejection reflex"—the automatic rejection of proposals simply because they have been previously rejected in other circumstances.

The SAVE approach compels thoughtful attention to *all* the factors involved in a prospective venture, thus preventing overvaluing the importance of a few dominant considerations.

SAVE provides a means of gathering, organizing, and utilizing the important major assets of any firm—collective observation, experience, and judgment—and applying them to some of the most difficult problems encountered anywhere in business.

SAVE provides the means for pinpointing and quantifying strengths and weaknesses, both present and potential. It also shows precisely where additional information is needed—specifically, where confidence levels are dangerously low—thus avoiding the waste motion and expense involved in conventional approaches which undertake to "find out the whole story," and then gather and sift through a ton of facts to obtain a pound of meaning.

SAVE significantly reduces the chances of venture failure by flagging the potential causes of failure in the very beginning. Even if management has already decided to proceed with a given venture, this pitfall-flagging property would be an extremely valuable tool in planning, implementing, and monitoring the undertaking. Forewarned is forearmed.

SAVE enables a firm to obtain a practical maximum value from consulting assistance should it be required, by pointing out the specific areas in which capabilities are weak and additional expertise is needed.

In looking at any successful business venture, there are always several obvious factors to which its success can be attributed. Competitors will attempt to duplicate the success by copying these obvious factors, and will fail. While there are several obvious success factors in any business, there are dozens of factors, equally important, that are not obvious; they cannot be copied because they are known only to the innovator. The SAVE analysis provides the way to assess both the obvious and the not-so-obvious factors that will ultimately determine the success of the new business venture.

Test yourself.

Pick out any planning problem.

Do you have good means of determining what your company or organization, or you yourself, already know about it?

Do you have good means of

- collecting this knowledge?
- articulating it?
- evaluating it?
- interpreting it?
- applying it to the problem?

The SAVE approach may be the way.

Appendices

Appendix I
The 69 SAVE Factors

I. Item Factors

A. Performance. How well does it work?
1. *Effectiveness.* Does it do its intended job well?
2. *Reliability.* Does it perform consistently, dependably, and safely?
3. *Simplicity.* How efficient and uncomplicated is it?
4. *Convenience.* Physically, how easy is it to install, use, store, and/or repair?

B. Salability. How well will it sell?
1. *Appearance.* Is it physically and/or functionally attractive?
2. *Uniqueness.* Does it have important exclusive features and talking points capable of supporting strong promotion?
3. *Economy.* How does its cost (to buy, install, operate, maintain, etc.) compare with competition?
4. *Timeliness.* Is this an opportune time for it?
5. *Understandability.* Can its functions and merits be easily and quickly understood by potential users?
6. *Tradability.* How well adapted to the proposed trade is it?
7. *Buyability.* To what extent does the buyer feel a conscious need for it at the point of sale?

C. Defensibility. To what extent can the company maintain its exclusivity and defend it against direct competition?
1. *Legal.* How firmly are its important features protected by patents, copyrights, trademarks, licenses, titles, franchises, or other legal means?
2. *Newness.* Does it have much of a "jump" on competition from the standpoint of development time?
3. *Proprietary.* Does it enjoy special advantages such as captive supplies, captive sales, process secrets, brand preference, or a strong line of companion items?

II. **Company Factors**

A. **Marketing. Does the company have what it takes to market this item effectively?**
1. *Experience.* How well does the company know the market and understand how to reach, sell, and service it?
2. *Support Services.* How does the company compare with average competition in order handling, warehousing, delivery time, freight expense, complaint adjustments, sales analysis, and so forth?
3. *Technical Service.* How does the company compare with average competition in terms of technical sales support?
4. *Market Coverage.* How completely does the company presently cover the market?
5. *Entrenchment.* How strong is the company's present trade and customer loyalty in this field?
6. *Dependency.* To what extent does the company's applicable marketing strength depend upon just a few individuals or accounts?
7. *Volume.* What was the company's volume in associated items last year, related to total sales?
8. *Penetration.* What is the company's approximate share of the total market for associated items?
9. *Management.* Is the company well situated for this item in terms of sales management?

B. **Technology. To what extent does the company have the technical know-how required for success here?**
1. *Design.* How does the company's design competence compare with competition?
2. *Engineering.* How does the company compare with competition in terms of engineering and problem-solving capabilities?
3. *Materials.* How well does the company know the materials involved in this item?
4. *Techniques.* How competitive is the company in terms of fabrication methods, systems, and process techniques?

C. **Production. Can the company produce the item competitively?**
1. *Labor.* How does the company's present labor situation compare with competition?
2. *Facilities.* How does the company compare with competition in terms of plant efficiency, equipment, automation, flexibility, and so forth?
3. *Purchasing.* How does the company compare with competition in terms of accessibility and prices of raw materials, supplies, and services required?
4. *Dependency.* To what extent is the company's production capability dependent upon just a few individuals?
5. *Capacity.* Does the company presently have the capacity to produce this item?

6. *Location.* How competitively located is the company?
7. *Management.* Is the company's production management well suited to handling this item?

III.   Environment Factors

A.   Market. Is there a strong market for this item?

1. *Potential Volume.* How large was last year's national market for similar items that are realistically displaceable by this item?
2. *Proportion.* How large is the anticipated market volume in proportion to the company's current total sales volume?
3. *Fertility.* What share of this market volume would the proposed item displace at a saturation level of marketing effort (not limited by cost) in all areas?
4. *Growth.* How much is the market expanding each year?
5. *Stability.* How constant is the demand?
6. *Outlook.* How great and enduring is the future demand for such items?

B.   Competition. What kind of competition dominates this market?

1. *Size.* How large is the typical competitor compared with the company?
2. *Specialization.* To what extent are other firms specializing in this item to the exclusion of companion items?
3. *Entrenchment.* How deeply entrenched in the trade are the competitors?
4. *Pricing.* How favorable is the traditional price behavior in this market?
5. *Entry Reaction.* What kind of competitive counteraction will your entry into this field probably cause?

C.   Suppliers. Is the industry well situated for supplies and services?

1. *Materials.* Are the required supplies and components readily and consistently available in the desired qualities and quantities at reasonable prices?
2. *Equipment.* Is the required equipment always readily available?
3. *Services.* How well supported is the industry in terms of available services—information, transportation, printing, equipment, repair, finishing, and so forth?
4. *Dependency.* To what extent are the industry's costs and operations dependent upon uncontrollable supply and/or service factors?

D.   Government. How might government be expected to affect this venture?

1. *Regulations.* How burdensome are government controls or rulings likely to be?
2. *Taxes.* To what extent will special tax considerations affect this venture?

3. *Programs.* To what extent will current or imminent government programs directly or indirectly affect the venture?
4. *Politics.* How is the political situation expected to influence this venture?

IV.   VENTURE FACTORS

A   **Support. How strongly supported is the venture?**
1. *Chief Executive.* To what extent does the chief executive sponsor the proposal?
2. *Management Group.* Does the operating management group support the proposal?
3. *Trade.* To what extent do the company's key agents, distributors, and dealers support the proposal?
4. *Customers.* To what extent do customers (or key prospects) endorse the venture?

B.   **Investment. Is this a good investment?**
1. *Size.* What is the total venture cost as a percentage of net worth?
2. *Commitment.* What percentage of the total venture cost is already committed?
3. *Maturity Rate.* How long will it take for sales volume to reach substantially full development?
4. *Risk.* How would the investment risk be classified?
5. *Return.* What is the estimated annual rate of return (on a present value or discounted cash flow basis)?
6. *Salvability.* If the venture should fail, what portion of the total investment could be salvaged or converted to cash?

C.   **Strategy. How well does the proposed venture serve the company's overall interests?**
1. *Consistency.* To what extent is the venture consistent or compatible with the company's goals, policies, obligations, and image?
2. *Appropriateness.* How appropriate is this venture as a company undertaking?
3. *Improvement.* To what extent will this venture improve the company and strengthen its overall position?
4. *Preemption.* To what extent would pursuit of this venture preempt other promising opportunities which are open to the company?
5. *Necessity.* To what extent is this venture really necessary for the company?
6. *Intuition.* Intuitively, how do you feel about the overall chances of success in this venture?

Appendix II
Forms Used in Strategic Analysis

Factor	Factor Rating	Factor Weight	Factor Score	Factor Group	Factor Group Score
Effectiveness	_____	_____	_____		
Reliability	_____	_____	_____		
Simplicity	_____	_____	_____	Performance	_____
Convenience	_____	_____	_____		
Appearance	_____	_____	_____		
Uniqueness	_____	_____	_____		
Economy	_____	_____	_____		
Timeliness	_____	_____	_____	Salability	_____
Understandability	_____	_____	_____		
Tradability	_____	_____	_____		
Buyability	_____	_____	_____		
Legal	_____	_____	_____		
Newness	_____	_____	_____	Defensibility	_____
Proprietary	_____	_____	_____		
Total Item Score					_____
Total Score Possible					_____
Item Efficiency Percentage					_____

Fig. AII-1. SAVE rating sheet for item factors.

Factor	Factor Rating	Factor Weight	Factor Score	Factor Group	Factor Group Score
Experience	_____	_____	_____		
Support Services	_____	_____	_____		
Technical Service	_____	_____	_____		
Market Coverage	_____	_____	_____		
Entrenchment	_____	_____	_____	Marketing	_____
Dependency	_____	_____	_____		
Volume	_____	_____	_____		
Penetration	_____	_____	_____		
Management	_____	_____	_____		
Design	_____	_____	_____		
Engineering	_____	_____	_____	Technology	_____
Materials	_____	_____	_____		
Techniques	_____	_____	_____		
Labor	_____	_____	_____		
Facilities	_____	_____	_____		
Purchasing	_____	_____	_____		
Dependency	_____	_____	_____	Production	_____
Capacity	_____	_____	_____		
Location	_____	_____	_____		
Management	_____	_____	_____		

Total Company Score   _____
Total Score Possible   _____
Company Efficiency Percentage   _____

Fig. AII-2. SAVE rating sheet for company factors.

Factor	Factor Rating	Factor Weight	Factor Score	Factor Group	Factor Group Score
Perseverance	_____	_____	_____		
Energy	_____	_____	_____		
Enthusiasm	_____	_____	_____	Personal	
Leadership	_____	_____	_____	Traits	_____
Character	_____	_____	_____		
Disposition	_____	_____	_____		
Intelligence	_____	_____	_____		
Management	_____	_____	_____		
Salesmanship	_____	_____	_____		
Materials	_____	_____	_____		
Equipment	_____	_____	_____	Know-How	_____
Techniques	_____	_____	_____		
Judgment	_____	_____	_____		
Education	_____	_____	_____		
Venture Savvy	_____	_____	_____		
Influence	_____	_____	_____		
Key Employees	_____	_____	_____	Additional	
Credit Standing	_____	_____	_____	Strengths	_____
Reputation	_____	_____	_____		
Other	_____	_____	_____		

Total Venturer Score   _____
Total Score Possible   _____
Venturer Efficiency Percentage   _____

Fig. AII-3. SAVE rating sheet for venturer factors.

Factor	Factor Rating	Factor Weight	Factor Score	Factor Group	Factor Group Score
Volume	_____	_____	_____		
Proportion	_____	_____	_____		
Fertility	_____	_____	_____	Market	_____
Growth	_____	_____	_____		
Stability	_____	_____	_____		
Outlook	_____	_____	_____		
Size	_____	_____	_____		
Specialization	_____	_____	_____		
Entrenchment	_____	_____	_____	Competition	_____
Pricing	_____	_____	_____		
Entry Reaction	_____	_____	_____		
Materials	_____	_____	_____		
Equipment	_____	_____	_____	Suppliers	_____
Services	_____	_____	_____		
Dependency	_____	_____	_____		
Regulations	_____	_____	_____		
Taxes	_____	_____	_____	Government	_____
Programs	_____	_____	_____		
Politics	_____	_____	_____		

Total Environment Score _____
Total Score Possible _____
Environment Efficiency Percentage _____

Fig. AII-4. SAVE rating sheet for environment factors.

Factor	Factor Rating	Factor Weight	Factor Score	Factor Group	Factor Group Score
Chief Executive	_____	_____	_____		
Management Group	_____	_____	_____	Support	_____
Trade	_____	_____	_____		
Customers	_____	_____	_____		
Size	_____	_____	_____		
Commitment	_____	_____	_____		
Maturity Rate	_____	_____	_____	Investment	_____
Risk	_____	_____	_____		
Return	_____	_____	_____		
Salvability	_____	_____	_____		
Consistency	_____	_____	_____		
Appropriateness	_____	_____	_____		
Improvement	_____	_____	_____	Strategy	_____
Preemption	_____	_____	_____		
Necessity	_____	_____	_____		
Intuition	_____	_____	_____		
Total Venture Score					_____
Total Score Possible					_____
Venture Efficiency Percentage					_____

Fig. AII-5. SAVE rating sheet for venture factors.

Factor Group	1 to 10 Rating	Factor Group Weight	Weighted Factor Group Score	Weighted Major Aspect Score	Maximum Possible Score	Efficiency Percentage
Performance	———	———	———			
Salability	———	———	———			
Defensibility	———	———	———	Item	———————	———
Marketing	———	———	———			
Technology	———	———	———			
Production	———	———	———	Company	———————	———
Market	———	———	———			
Competition	———	———	———			
Suppliers	———	———	———	Environment		
Government	———	———	———			
Support	———	———	———			
Investment	———	———	———			
Strategy	———	———	———	Venture	———————	———
Total Screening Rating				———————	———

Fig. AII-6. SAVE preliminary screening analysis.

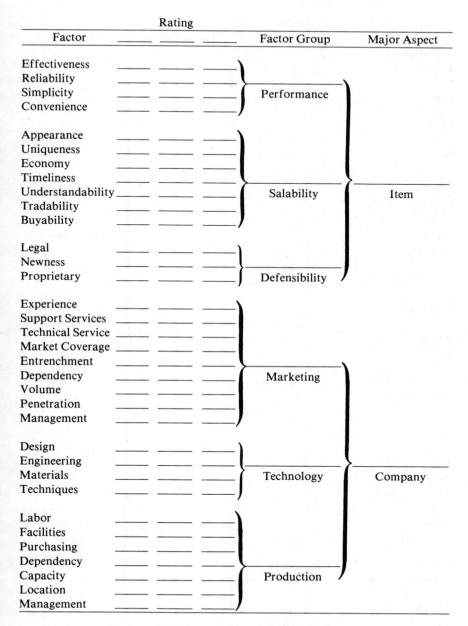

Factor	Rating			Factor Group	Major Aspect

Factor	Rating	Factor Group	Major Aspect
Effectiveness			
Reliability			
Simplicity	Performance		
Convenience			
Appearance			
Uniqueness			
Economy			
Timeliness			
Understandability	Salability	Item	
Tradability			
Buyability			
Legal			
Newness			
Proprietary	Defensibility		
Experience			
Support Services			
Technical Service			
Market Coverage			
Entrenchment			
Dependency	Marketing		
Volume			
Penetration			
Management			
Design			
Engineering			
Materials	Technology	Company	
Techniques			
Labor			
Facilities			
Purchasing			
Dependency			
Capacity	Production		
Location			
Management			

Fig. AII-7. Strategic analysis for venture evaluation.
SAVE 69-Factor Rating Sheet (Page 1 of 2)

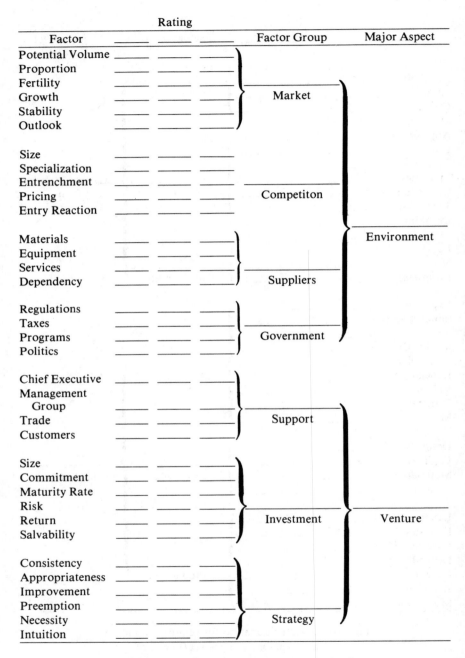

Fig. AII-7. Strategic analysis for venture evaluation.
SAVE 69-Factor Rating Sheet (Page 2 of 2)

Factor Group	Maximum Possible Score	Actual Score	Efficiency Percentage
Item Factors			
Performance	_____	_____	_____
Salability	_____	_____	_____
Defensibility	_____	_____	_____
Total	_____	_____	_____
Company Factors			
Marketing	_____	_____	_____
Technology	_____	_____	_____
Production	_____	_____	_____
Total	_____	_____	_____
Environment Factors			
Market	_____	_____	_____
Competition	_____	_____	_____
Suppliers	_____	_____	_____
Government	_____	_____	_____
Total	_____	_____	_____
Venture Factors			
Support	_____	_____	_____
Investment	_____	_____	_____
Strategy	_____	_____	_____
Total	_____	_____	_____
Total Venture	_____	_____	_____

Fig. AII-8. Summary Sheet—SAVE analysis for proposed venture.

Appendix III
Case History

Snark Enterprise Inc.

The following case history describes a SAVE analysis for a small company's proposed new product venture. It is an actual study conducted by and for a real situation and uses real data. The company's decisions and actions were based on the results of this study. Only the owner's and company's name have been changed.

COMPANY HISTORY

Snark Enterprise Inc. was started in 1975 by Gravely P. Snark, a college professor. Mr. Snark, a highly creative and innovative individual with strong entrepreneurial inclinations, developed an interest in 4-wheel drive (4WD) and off-road vehicles. Recognizing some of the problems existing in original and after-market equipment, as well as in the available service facilities, Mr. Snark resigned his university post. Using his savings and whatever could be borrowed from friends and relatives, he formed Snark Enterprise Inc. Equity interests were later sold to two outside investors—both having good business backgrounds and a strong interest in this particular business—with Mr. Snark maintaining a majority interest.

The company had two distinct operations: (1) a service shop specializing in all services for 4WD vehicles, from special-purpose customizing to minor repairs and tune-ups and (2) a manufacturing operation, offering a high-quality, premium-priced fiberglass top for specific 4WD vehicles. The truck top was designed and developed by Mr. Snark; sales were primarily direct to the consumer, reached through mail order and direct mail advertising. The company showed annual sales of about $300,000. The service business showed modest profits, while the manufacturing/sales business was operating at about a break-even level.

A new venture was obviously needed to take advantage of the company's considerable technical capabilities and its already-developed markets. It was felt that the right kind of project could greatly increase sales, without significantly increasing marketing expenses, thus putting the manufacturing segment of the business in a highly profitable position.

VENTURE DESCRIPTION

Two alternatives for a new venture became quickly apparent:

1. Additional truck tops, similar to the ones already being manufactured, for other truck makes or models.
2. Lower priced tops for larger markets, with the possibility of offering the new products through large national merchandisers and mail-order catalog houses.

Through the creative efforts of Mr. Snark and his associates, an approach was developed to exploit both avenues simultaneously. The premium quality truck top consisted of two separate fiberglass skins (the interior and exterior surfaces), with insulating material sandwiched between. By employing some innovative design and production changes, a method was devised by which one of the two separate skins of the premium truck top could be used by itself as the budget truck top, thus minimizing the investment and inventory, and eliminating the need for additional pattern and mold making.

Despite the apparent attractiveness of this new venture, additional capital was needed to pursue its development. Since commercial banks generally loan money to a company such as this based on its past rather than its potential, additional outside investors were sought. One of the prospective investors, a particularly shrewd engineer and businessman, requested that a strategic audit be conducted prior to making any major financial commitments.

This SAVE analysis, then, is aimed specifically at identifying the chances of success for the new products to be manufactured and marketed by the company.

RATING THE 69 FACTORS

The SAVE evaluation was performed by three of the individuals intimately involved both in the existing operations and in the proposed venture, under the overall supervision of an outside consultant. Each participant went through the 69 factors independently. Their ratings for each of the factors are recorded on the 69-factor rating sheet shown in Fig. AIII-1.

The three persons selected to evaluate the proposed venture (identified as A, B, and C on the rating sheet) were: (A) the production manager, (B) the president, and (C) the treasurer. As might be expected, the chief executive was the most optimistic of the three, while the financial officer showed the least enthusiasm. The production manager rated product performance and the company's technological and production capabilities highly, while the president (who also functions as sales manager) ranked the venture highly in terms of product salability, marketing capabilities, and most other factors. The treasurer assigned the lowest ratings of the three in almost every factor group.

ANALYZING THE RAW SCORES

Taking the three sets of raw rating scores, the analysis can proceed in several different ways, depending on whatever types of information management needs from the study.

1. Each of the three sets of ratings can be analyzed separately, resulting in three sets of venture scores.
2. The three sets of ratings could be averaged, and the single "average" set used in further computations.
3. The high, middle, and low ratings for each factor could be used to develop a range of values, from which an expected value and variance could be computed.
4. The median or middle rating for each factor could be used as a representative value in completing the analysis.

Rating

Factor	A	B	C	Factor Group	Major Aspect
Effectiveness	10	10	10		
Reliability	10	9	8	37 32 29	
Simplicity	10	8	8	Performance	
Convenience	7	5	3		
Appearance	10	10	10		
Uniqueness	10	10	10		
Economy	4	4	2		
Timeliness	7	7	5	45 55 50	100 109 97
Under-standability	3	7	6	Salability	Item
Tradability	5	7	8		
Buyability	6	10	9		
Legality	5	7	6		
Newness	6	9	7	18 22 18	
Proprietary	7	6	5	Defensibility	
Experience	7	8	3		
Support Services	1	6	1		
Technical Service	2	4	5		
Market Coverage	5	8	3		
Entrenchment	8	8	7	44 64 41	
Dependency	7	8	5	Marketing	
Volume	2	5	4		
Penetration	7	9	8		
Management	5	8	5		
Design	10	10	6		
Engineering	8	8	5	34 34 24	123 137 103
Materials	9	8	6	Technology	Company
Techniques	7	8	7		
Labor	8	9	5		
Facilities	7	5	8		
Purchasing	6	6	3		
Dependency	6	5	7	45 39 38	
Capacity	6	5	5	Production	
Location	4	2	5		
Management	8	7	5		

Fig. AIII-1. Strategic analysis for venture evaluation.
SAVE 69-Factor Rating Sheet (Page 1 of 2)

Rating

Factor	A	B	C	Factor Group	Major Aspect
Potential Volume	6	4	5		
Proportion	2	8	10		
Fertility	6	7	1		
Growth	8	7	5	33 36 29	
Stability	4	5	3	Market	
Outlook	7	5	5		
Size	6	9	5		
Specialization	8	8	6		
Entrenchment	8	7	5	36 34 28	
Pricing	6	5	5	Competition	
Entry Reaction	8	5	7		117 113 112
					Environment
Materials	5	5	5		
Equipment	9	8	5	26 23 20	
Services	7	8	5	Suppliers	
Dependency	5	2	5		
Regulations	7	5	5		
Taxes	5	5	5	22 20 18	
Programs	5	5	4	Government	
Politics	5	5	4		
Chief Executive	10	10	10		
Management Group	10	10	8	36 38 29	
Trade	8	8	5	Support	
Customers	8	10	6		
Size	3	1	3		
Commitment	5	9	10		
Maturity Rate	7	8	7	26 35 23	116 131 100
Risk	5	3	1	Investment	Venture
Return	5	9	1		
Salvability	1	5	1		
Consistency	10	10	8		
Appropriateness	10	10	8		
Improvement	10	10	8	54 58 48	
Preemption	7	9	8	Strategy	
Necessity	9	10	9		
Intuition	8	9	7		

Fig. AIII-1. Strategic analysis for venture evaluation.
SAVE 69-Factor Rating Sheet (Page 2 of 2)

The third approach would give the clearest picture of the new venture's potential; an approach like this would be especially good for a company having many such proposals to consider, providing a computer were available for handling the data.

For illustrative purposes here, though, the fourth approach was used. The middle of the three ratings for each factor—regardless of which of the three project participants assigned the rating—is entered in the "Factor Rating" column on the following four SAVE rating sheets.

Because of the manufacturer-to-consumer nature of this business, the business's characteristics combine elements of both the manufacturing industry and retail trade. Consequently, the factor weights are based on both manufacturing and retail elements. Six of the 13 factor groups are weighted for manufacturing: performance, defensibility, technology, production, suppliers, and investment. Five factor groups are weighted as a retail business: salability, marketing, market, competition, and strategy. The other two factor groups—

Factor	Factor Rating	Factor Weight	Factor Score	Factor Group	Factor Group Score
Effectiveness	10	1	10		
Reliability	9	1	9		
Simplicity	8	1	8	Performance	32
Convenience	5	1	5		
Appearance	10	1	10		
Uniqueness	10	1	10		
Economy	4	1	4		
Timeliness	7	1	7	Salability	82
Understandability	6	2	12		
Tradability	7	3	21		
Buyability	9	2	18		
Legality	6	1	6		
Newness	7	1	7	Defensibility	19
Proprietary	6	1	6		
Total Item Score					133
Total Score Possible					180
Item Efficiency Percentage					73.9

Fig. AIII-2. SAVE rating sheet for item factors.

Factor	Factor Rating	Factor Weight	Factor Score	Factor Group	Factor Group Score
Experience	7	2	14		
Support Services	1	1	1		
Technical Service	4	1	4		
Market Coverage	5	1	5		
Entrenchment	8	2	16	Marketing	64
Dependency	7	1	7		
Volume	4	1	4		
Penetration	8	1	8		
Management	5	1	5		
Design	10	1	10		
Engineering	8	1	8	Technology	33
Materials	8	1	8		
Techniques	7	1	7		
Labor	8	1	8		
Facilities	7	1	7		
Purchasing	6	1	6		
Dependency	6	1	6	Production	43
Capacity	5	1	5		
Location	4	1	4		
Management	7	1	7		
Total Company Score					140
Total Score Possible					220
Company Efficiency Percentage					63.6

Fig. AIII-3. SAVE rating sheet for company factors.

government and support—are weighted the same in both manufacturing and retail businesses.

The appropriate weights are entered in the "Factor Weight" column, and the factor score is calculated as the product of factor rating and factor weight. The resulting factor scores are totaled by factor groups, and the totals entered as the "Factor Group Score". The total score is simply the sum of the factor group scores, while the "Total Score Possible" amounts to ten times the sum of the factor weights. Finally, the overall efficiency percentage is calculated by dividing the "Total Score" by the "Total Score Possible."

Factor	Factor Rating	Factor Weight	Factor Score	Factor Group	Factor Group Score
Volume	5	1	5		
Proportion	8	1	8		
Fertility	6	1	6	Market	39
Growth	7	1	7		
Stability	4	2	8		
Outlook	5	1	5		
Size	6	2	12		
Specialization	8	2	16		
Entrenchment	7	1	7	Competition	52
Pricing	5	2	10		
Entry Reaction	7	1	7		
Materials	5	1	5		
Equipment	8	1	8	Suppliers	25
Services	7	1	7		
Dependency	5	1	5		
Regulations	5	1	5		
Taxes	5	1	5	Government	20
Programs	5	1	5		
Politics	5	1	5		
Total Environment Score					136
Total Score Possible					230
Environment Efficiency Percentage					59.1

Fig. AIII-4. SAVE rating sheet for environment factors.

SUMMARY AND CONCLUSIONS

The data from the preceding four rating sheets can then be brought together on the following Summary Sheet (Fig. AIII-6). The calculations are the same as before, with efficiency percentages calculated for each of the 13 factor groups and for the venture as a whole.

Efficiency percentages can be seen to range from a low of 50.0 on government factors to a high of 90.0 for venture support and strategy. Overall, the total venture earns a 67.3 percent efficiency rating.

Factor	Factor Rating	Factor Weight	Factor Score	Factor Group	Factor Group Score
Chief Executive	10	1	10		
Management Group	10	1	10	Support	36
Trade	8	1	8		
Customers	8	1	8		
Size	3	1	3		
Commitment	9	1	9		
Maturity Rate	7	1	7	Investment	28
Risk	3	1	3		
Return	5	1	5		
Salvability	1	1	1		
Consistency	10	1	10		
Appropriateness	10	1	10		
Improvement	10	1	10	Strategy	72
Preemption	8	1	8		
Necessity	9	2	18		
Intuition	8	2	16		
Total Venture Score					136
Total Score Possible					180
Venture Efficiency Percentage					75.6

Fig. AIII-5. SAVE rating sheet for venture factors.

The guidelines for venture acceptability proposed in Chapter 7 called for a minimum rating of 3 on individual factors and efficiency ratings of 40 percent minimum on the 13 factor groups, 50 percent on the 4 major facets, and 60 percent on the total venture.

This proposed venture has only 2 individual factors falling below the suggested minimum: support services and investment salvability, both of which the chief executive had rated much higher. All 13 factor groups are well above the guideline minimum, as are the 4 major facets and the venture as a whole.

In view of the many strengths and few weaknesses associated with this proposed venture opportunity, the obvious conclusion was to actively pursue it.

Factor Group	Maximum Possible Score	Actual Score	Efficiency Percentage
Item Factors			
Performance	40	32	80.0
Salability	110	82	74.5
Defensibility	30	19	63.3
Total	180	133	73.9
Company Factors			
Marketing	110	64	58.2
Technology	40	33	82.5
Production	70	43	61.4
Total	220	140	63.6
Environment Factors			
Market	70	39	55.7
Competition	80	52	65.0
Suppliers	40	25	62.5
Government	40	20	50.0
Total	230	136	59.1
Venture Factors			
Support	40	36	90.0
Investment	60	28	46.7
Strategy	80	72	90.0
Total	180	136	75.6
Total Venture	810	545	67.3

Fig. AIII-6. Summary sheet—SAVE analysis for proposed venture.

Index

Index